The Advanced Stock Market Investing Guide

Follow This Step by Step Beginners Trading Guide for Learning How to Trade Penny Stocks, Bonds, Options, Forex, and Shares; to Become a Stock Trader Today!

By Neil Sharp

Table of Contents

Introduction

Congratulations on purchasing "***The Advanced Stock Market Investing Guide*** : *Follow This Step by Step Beginners Trading Guide for Learning How to Trade Penny Stocks, Bonds, Options, Forex, and Shares; to Become a Stock Trader Today!*" Great care was taken in ensuring that the information contained herein is not only useful but relevant.

The following pages contain a trove of actionable information and advice which the average individual can put into practice in order to become a stock trader. Since this is a rather extensive topic, the contents of each chapter have been boiled down to their essence. This means that there is no fluff; just the good stuff.

Also, great care has been taken to ensure that the concepts described throughout this book are explained in a clear, plain language that is devoid of complicated business jargon. As such, this book isn't about sounding smart – it's about actually being smart!

I am sure that you have chosen this book because you are interested in finding out how you can make more money than you are today. And there is nothing wrong with that! In fact, I commend your desire to earn a better living and provide a higher quality of life for your loved ones.

The main objective of this book is to provide you with a guide filled with relevant information that will allow you to become a stock trader and actually make money.

If you are looking for practice examples of how financial markets work, then you have come to the right place.

Each chapter covers one fundamental area of stock trading.

First, we will take a close look at the importance of investing and how you can make money in financial markets by choosing your investments wisely.

Then, we will have an in-depth discussion of the different investment vehicles available to you. This means that you will learn about how these investments work, the pitfalls that come with them, and how you can make money.

Next, we will look into day trading. This is a key chapter since it will enable you to get a good sense of what it takes to become a stock trader. Through analysis and insight, you will be able to make up your mind and decide if day trading is for you.

If you feel that day trading isn't your thing, there are also two chapters based on investment strategies that you can implement without actually getting your hands dirty. These strategies are meant to put your money to work without taking up too much of your time.

Also, we will discuss how legislation and taxes can play a role in your investment strategy. In particular, we will have an in-depth discussion on how reckless investment practices led to the financial crisis of 2008.

Finally, we will go over the lives of some of the most famous investor in history. The stories of these individuals are meant to inspire you, but also provide you with role models that you can emulate. These are not flamboyant traders like those seen in Hollywood movies. These are ordinary folks that made it big through hard work and savvy investment.

So, what are you waiting for?

Let's jump right in and learn how to become a stock trader today!

Chapter 1: The Importance of Investing

"Money doesn't grow on trees."

Have you ever heard that expression? I'm sure you have.

And, it's true.

Nevertheless, money does grow, just in a different sense.

Most folks obtain money through their jobs. When a person gets a job, they are compensated for the work they do. Whatever the work that is done, the person receives a sum of money in exchange.

That money is then used to acquire the goods and services needed in order to live. Some folks manage to save some of their earnings at the end of the month, some break even, and some are in a hole.

This cycle of working for money ties the earnings of an individual to their work. So, the more they work, the more they earn at least in theory.

Some folks choose to go through life working, paying their taxes and perhaps collecting a pension at the end of their career.

Other folks choose to blow all their money and end up poor at the end of their productive lives.

Other folks choose to invest part of their money.

In economic terms, investing is the result of saving. When a person saves money, that surplus amount of money is eligible for investment since the person doesn't actually need to spend. If they did, then they wouldn't have saved it.

Unless an individual chooses to dig a hole in the ground and bury their savings, money tends to find its way to investors.

One simple example of this is leaving money in the bank.

The money that is deposited into a bank account will make its way to investors through what is called "fractional reserve lending."

This concept indicates that the money that is deposited by customers into a bank is eligible to be loaned out to other customers. So, when a customer comes to the bank and asks for a loan, the bank can loan out the money deposited by the other customers.

By law, banks are required to keep a fraction of that money in the vault for customers who want to make a withdrawal. Hence, fractional reserve lending means that banks must keep a small part of their customers' deposits and may loan out the rest.

This is a simple example of how savings translate into investment.

On the whole, investment is needed to drive a country's economy. Under a capitalist system, the more money circulates, the more good and services change hands. In addition, the more money that ends up in people's pockets.

That's why burying your savings in the backyard will kill any economic momentum.

As an individual, investing represents an opportunity to make money grow literally.

The most commonly known type of investment is a bank account.

Bank accounts will pay an amount of money called "interest" calculated on how much money a customer has deposited in that bank.

Other common types of investments are 401(k)'s or even businesses. These investments use money to make more money.

A 401(k) is essentially a bank account in which an employee contributes money to it every month. The financial institution that secures the 401(k) will take that money and invest it in other ventures. The money that financial institution makes is what is used to pay off the interest accrued by that 401(k).

If an individual chooses to invest in a business, the profits earned from that business will also make money grow.

Over time, money invested may generate enough income to a point where it can fund a person's lifestyle. This is the main purpose of saving up for retirement. You may also hear about those individuals who have "retired early."

In essence, retiring means that you no longer have to work in order to finance your lifestyle. And this can be done through investing.

Now, that takes us into what is known as the stock market.

The stock market, or financial markets for that matter, enable individual investors to take their money and put it to work. The series of financial instruments and vehicles available to investors allows them to earn money from placing their surplus earnings in the hands of individuals who will make use of that money.

By investing in the stock market, investors are not looking to pursue business opportunities that imply the production of goods and services. These are speculative activities that are based on "paper assets." In other words, there are no tangible objects at play. Rather, the investments made are in buying and selling assets which will produce a yield.

This yield is basically the profits made on investments in financial markets.

For those individuals who seek to secure their future, grow their net worth or achieve the lifestyle they have always dreamed about, then investing in financial markets is a plausible way of achieving this.

However, investing in financial markets is no easy task for those who don't know what they are doing. For those who do, they are able to navigate the waters of the system and use it to their advantage.

Of course, becoming an expert at trading in financial markets takes some time and training. But with the right coaching and information, becoming an expert is a lot easier than you might think. The important thing is to have the willingness to put in the time and effort it takes to learn.

The benefits of investing outweigh the risks by far as long as you know what you are doing. This is why investing in the stock market is not recommended for individuals who do not have the know-how and are not willing to seek qualified financial advice.

But by reading this guide, you will be able to take your own investment strategy and maximize your chances at making it.

Will you be the next Wall Street millionaire?

Maybe!

And I use the word "maybe" because it's up to you to make the right choices based on accurate information, a strong "gut" and common sense.

In the next chapter, we will take a closer look at how financial markets work.

Chapter 2: Stock Market Fundamentals

The words "stock market" are two of the most magical words in the English language.

To some, the stock market has been a source of great wealth and opportunity. To others, these words have meant headaches and stress.

The fact of the matter is that much of the stress and anxiety that comes from investing in the stock market comes from a lack of understanding into its nature. Often, you will hear much information and advice regarding the stocks and other financial assets. However, the so-called experts and pundits on television do little to actually explain the fundamentals of investing.

Investing in financial markets does not have to become stressful, even if it may be painful at times. With the right understanding of how financial markets work, you can begin to invest wisely and successfully. That is why it is necessary to lay some groundwork.

In this chapter, we will cover the basics and fundamentals of financial markets. We will take a deep look into definitions of the most important concepts pertaining to investing in financial markets. Moreover, the information contained herein should be considered as a guide, a road map if you will, on how to navigate through the various investment vehicles and instruments available to the average investor.

It is important to note that this chapter is not so much about providing financial advice on what the best investment vehicles are, but rather, it is about having a holistic approach on the various types of financial assets at the disposal of the average investor.

Also, it is worth noting that the term "average investor" refers to a regular individual who is looking to put some of the hard-earned cash into equities, bonds or any other assets. We are not considering the large, institutional investors, such as investment banks of hedge funds, as they play under different rules and circumstances.

As such, the average investor is someone who is looking to take advantage of the opportunities the market affords and multiply their savings into a greater amount that can serve as income down the road. Furthermore, large, institutional investors dabble in derivates markets. This is something that we will refer to throughout this book, but we will not be touching upon in too much detail as we are focused on getting you off the ground.

So, buckle up. This chapter is filled with concepts, definitions, and above all, actionable information which will surely open your eyes into the realm of possibilities available in the stock market. Most importantly, you will be able to form your own, informed opinion about what is available to you as an average investor. That way, you can begin planning your investment strategy right off the bat!

Definition of financial markets

The stock market, or equities market, is one of several different markets that make up a greater sum known as "financial markets."

In essence, financial markets are a place (either physical or virtual) where lenders, investors, borrowers, and buyers come together to buy and sell equities, securities, derivatives, commodities, bonds or financial assets such as mutual funds or exchange-traded funds (ETFs).

Let's take a closer look at each item:

• **Equities**: These are shares of publicly traded companies that are available on major indices such as the Dow Jones, Nasdaq and the S&P 500 in the United States. There are also other major financial markets throughout the world in countries such as Japan, Germany, Spain, and the UK.

• **Securities**: The are debt instruments which lenders can package and sell to investors. For example, banks can package mortgages and sell them to hedge funds who get a return on their investment from the interest paid by borrowers.

• **Derivative**: These are complex financial instruments mainly available to institutional investors. Derivates, as its name suggests, are instruments which are "derived" from an underlying asset. These instruments are often high-risk and may represent a high-risk, high reward proposition for investors.

• **Commodities**: These are investments into physical goods such as oil, agricultural products, precious metals or any other physical good produced by companies.

• **Mutual funds**: This is a pool of money collected by a financial institution from investors which is then used to buy and sell a portfolio of financial assets. The return on the entire portfolio of investors is then distributed among the total pool of investors.

• **Exchange Traded Funds**: These funds are similar to mutual funds with the difference that there is an underlying asset to the fund. For instance, oil can be traded by way of an ETF. An investor can buy into an oil ETF and collect a return from the profits in oil prices.

• **Bonds**: These are debt instruments issued by sovereign governments or private corporations. The bond market is the biggest financial market in the world. Some countries, like the United States, allow private citizens to purchase government bonds while other countries sell them on international financial markets only to institutional investors.

The financial instruments mentioned above are called "paper assets" as they represent investments of cash into vehicles which are not physically tangible. Except for commodities, financial assets are essentially represented by certificates which are proof of ownership. Moreover, many of these investments are not represented by cold, hard cash, but rather, are represented by money in digital form.

ETFs for commodities such as oil, precious metals (gold and silver), industrial metals (copper, tin, aluminum), agricultural products (sugar, coffee, corn, cattle), or energy products (coal, natural gas) may or may not come along with a physical allocation. What that means is that if the ETF contract does not specify that the investor will take physical delivery of the commodity, then the investor will only receive a monetary payment corresponding to the investment made.

Conversely, when an ETF contract does specify a physical allocation, the investor may choose to take physical delivery of the commodity specified in the contract. So, the investor can cash out by receiving sacks of coffee instead of a check for the monetary amount indicated in the contract.

Now, let's move on to a more in-depth definition of each financial instrument.

Equities

Equities are the most-commonly known financial assets.

This is what is commonly referred to as the "stock market."

In essence, stocks are "shares" of a company which any investor can purchase. Each share is a proportion of ownership of that specific company. For example, if a company issues 1000 shares, then 50% ownership of that company would represent ownership of 500 shares. By the same token, one share represents ownership of that company, albeit in a minuscule proportion.

When a company is formed, corporate law requires it to be "incorporated." This means that the company must become a formal legal entity. This means that a regular "mom and pop" business does not qualify as it is most likely a sole proprietorship. Hence, small businesses do not fall into this category.

One thing about small business though: hedge funds invest in what is called "private equities." That means that they buy into companies which are not publicly traded. Think of "Shark Tank" when considering private equities. These are entrepreneurs or startup companies that have a significant value proposition which investors want to get into at its early stages so they can clean up when the company grows.

So, when a company reaches a point when they are large enough to draw considerable interest from larger, institutional investments such as hedge funds and investment banks (also sovereign wealth funds may throw their hat in the ring), the company will enter a process called its "initial public offering" or IPO.

In the IPO process, all of the owners of the company, which is still private, decide they will put their shares for sale to anyone who chooses to purchase them. The valuation of those shares depends on the company's profit outlook.

For instance, if ABC Company decides to "go public," the company must be valued. The actual book value of the company is irrelevant as investors are paying for the dividends they will earn per share. So, if the company is highly profitable, then the shareholders, at the time of the IPO, will have an asking price for their shares.

Let's say that the asking price is $100 per share. This asking price is tested in the market to gauge interest at that price point. If the company is red-hot, investors may signal, by word of mouth, if they are willing to pay that much, or even more. Also, investors may feel the valuation is too high, and they would be willing to pay less.

Next, an authorized broker, usually a large investment bank such as Merrill Lynch or JP Morgan in the United States, will "underwrite" the IPO. In other words, they will present ABC Company's shares to the market. This is like having a middle-man sell the shares of the company to investors.

Derivatives come into play here, since IPO underwriters must have another financial institution insure the IPO. The insurance needs to be included in case something goes wrong and the deal falls through. For example, fraudulent activity is discovered, or an event of significant impact disrupts the company's operations. As such, insurance protects investors' money going into the deal.

The entire IPO process is supervised by the Securities and Exchange Commission (SEC) in the United States in order to ensure that the entire process has been done according to regulations. Every country that has financial markets will have their own regulatory agency.

Once the IPO is ready, the company will enter one of the financial markets available in the world. Not all companies are traded in the United States. American companies may choose to be traded on international markets such as in London or Hong Kong. Companies from outside the United States may choose to be included in American stock exchanges.

Once the IPO has gone public, then the shares are up for sale. This is when brokerage firms and other investment institutions can choose to scoop up the shares. This is where the early investors clean up.

Let's assume that XYZ capital funded ABC Company and provided them with seed capital at its outset. They invested $10,000 in exchange for 100 shares. That works out to $100 a share. The IPO valuation of ABC Company was listed at $1,000 a share. When ABC Company went public, XYZ capital received $1000 per share when it originally paid $100.

This example is not uncommon but not frequent.

The average investor will jump into the race well after the IPO.

While shares of all publicly traded companies are technically available to anyone with the cash to invest, they are not always up for sale.

For instance, if XYZ Capital holds 100 shares of Apple, they may choose to simply sit on them and not sell. Perhaps they are waiting for the price to go up and then turn around and sell them. Or, the company has not posted strong earnings and XYZ Capital is waiting for Apple to rebound before deciding to sell.

This brings up to the next point: the price of shares on the open market is set by supply and demand.

In economic terms, demand is driven by the amount of money available to invest. This money comes from two main sources: the average investor, that is, mon and pop who have some extra money set aside and would like to put it to work, and institutional investors.

Institutional investors are hedge funds, investment banks or even sovereign wealth fund.

A hedge fund is a "club" of wealthy individuals who pool their money together. The hedge fund itself is a financial institution which is in charge of managing the money to the benefit of its members. Needless to say, hedge funds are thirsty for profits and will always demand higher yields, and higher returns. In addition, hedge funds tend to be cowboys, that is, they will take on the highest amount of risk, if and when, they pay off is commensurate to the risk.

Investment banks are more traditional financial institutions such as Merrill Lynch, or JP Morgan in the United States, or huge international banks such as HSBC, Scotiabank, Deutsche Bank, Credit Suisse to name a few. These aren't necessarily banks in the traditional sense of the word, that is, a savings and loan bank, but rather, these are formal wealth management companies that are governed by the prevailing financial regulations of the country in which they are incorporated.

Unlike investment banks, hedge funds often do not fall under the same regulatory umbrella. This is why they engage in higher-risk activities since many countries, especially in Europe, consider hedge funds to be private enterprises. Therefore, they are no different than a hardware store. The only difference is that they don't sell hammers. Instead, they sell financial assets.

Lastly, sovereign wealth funds are institutions which are represented by countries. These funds are generally state-owned institutions that have the official backing of a sovereign state. For example, the largest sovereign wealth fund in the world is China. Consequently, this is official Chinese state money which can be invested in equities, commodities and other financial vehicles. Not all countries have these funds, and most sovereign funds are not closely regulated by their country of origin.

The investment money available in a country, region or the entire world, will compete for the best investments. This competition is what drives up the price of the best investments available. This is why bonds are the largest financial market since they offer lower risk and almost guaranteed returns. The only way a bond cannot be repaid is if a country defaults on its debt such as the case of Argentina or Russia.

When available investment money enters the market, the best investments get snatched up first. But since other investors are looking to put their money to work, they might be willing to pay more for those very same investments. This is what drives up the price of a bond, stock, or even commodity.

Also, if a company falls flat and their earnings do not live up to investors' expectations, shareholders may choose to dump their shares in that company. That drives the price down as buyers may not be willing to pay the same amount of money for those shares. That may mean that current shareholders may take a loss or just a lesser profit.

Let's consider ABC Company. ABC Company's shares went up to $1000 per share after its IPO. It's a hot tech stock, and everybody wants in. The initial investors cleaned up they made a nice bit of change on the IPO.

It has come time for ABC Company to report its quarterly earnings. In their report, ABC Company reported higher-than-expected profits. This sends the stock soaring as everyone wants a piece of the action. The stock goes from $1000 to $1100 in a matter of minutes. In this case, demand from investors dries up the price as not all shareholders decide to sell. They want to hold on to the stock because it's doing so well. So, those who do decide to sell make a greater profit because there is a limited number of shares available. And, investors are going wild.

On the contrary, let's assume that ABC Company's earnings were lower than expected. This means that shareholders are now worried about what might happen to the company. They might choose to hold, hoping that it will rebound in the next quarter.

Other shareholders might think that the company is in trouble and decide they want to get out. They bought into ABC Company at $1000 a share. But because its earnings were lower than expected, buyers may choose to pay $900 a share. They figure they will buy low hoping that the company will rebound and make a profit in the next quarter. Those shareholders who bought at $1000 and sell at $900, have now taken a $100 per share hit.

As you can see, the forces of supply and demand are what drive the price of equities. Therefore, companies need to be careful they don't issue too many shares or else the price of each share will drop. Conversely, some companies engage in what is called "buybacks." This is when a company buys back its own stock. Since there is less of the stock available, the price will go up as investors will try to find more shares but will have to pay more for the existing ones.

Another item to consider is the definition of a stock exchange.

As mentioned earlier, there are many stock exchanges throughout the world. They belong to specific countries and are governed by the legislation of their home country.

In the United States, there are several stock exchanges.

- New York Stock Exchange (Wall Street)
- Chicago Stock Exchange
- Boston Stock Exchange
- Miami Stock Exchange
- Philadelphia Stock Exchange

Each one of these exchanges is a physical location where traders meet to buy and sell equities, commodities or other securities.

Most people often confuse stock exchanges with indices such as the Dow Jones and the Nasdaq. The difference is that the Dow and Nasdaq are not physical locations where traders meet to do business. They are merely statistical measures of one portion of the market.

For example, the Dow Jones measures the top 30 companies in the market. This measure tracks their performance and determines the trend for the market. The Nasdaq was the first computerized trading system that eventually became a stock market index. It generally tracks "tech" companies though it is not exclusive to this sector. Another index is the S&P 500 which is a measure of the top 500 companies which are not included in the Dow Jones.

At this point, it is important to take a look at the other financial assets available to investors.

Bonds

The bond market is perhaps the most important market in the world.

Bonds are certificates of debt which sovereign nations or private corporations issue. These instruments allow institutions to obtain funding on the promise that they will pay that money back, plus interest when the bond matures, that is, when the time is up.

There are several terms on bonds. They range from 30 days to 30 years. They come in all shapes and sizes since they respond to the needs of the institutions issuing them.

The interest that bonds pay out to buyers is called "yield." The issuer basically sets the yield, though it varies depending on market forces. The yield itself does not change. That is the interest that is paid on it. For example, if a bond has a $100 face value, a coupon of 10%, then the 10% would be considered the yield. Note that the coupon is calculated on the face value of the bond.

If the issuing county of that bond is a stable and solid state, then investors may choose to pay more than the $100 face value in order to purchase a safe asset. Let's assume that investors are willing to pay $110 for the $100 bond. Then considering the 10% coupon, that is, $10 worth of interest, then the yield would be calculated as 10/110 = 0.09 or 9%. This means the yield has fallen to 9%. The logic is that the safer the investment, the lower the yield.

On the other hand, this issuing country is having economic troubles and may not live up to their financial obligations. In other words, they are at risk of defaulting or not paying back their bonds. So, bondholders may choose to drop the bond like a hot potato. Bondholders will short, or sell for less, and take $90 on the $100 face value bond. This means that the yield has risen since the coupon is still 10%, but the price paid for the bond is less. Here is the calculation: 10/90 = 0.111 or 11.1%. The yield is now 11% because market logic dictates that the higher the risk, the higher the yield.

Sovereign governments may choose to place their bonds in the United States stock exchanges, or in any other stock exchange, they consider appropriate. And like equities or stocks, bonds must be underwritten by a reputable financial institution if they are placed in the United States. In other countries, the laws of that country govern the placement of bonds.

Bonds may also be insured. This insurance of bonds falls into the derivatives market as insurers are essentially betting that a country will or will not default on its debt obligations. If the country does default, then insurers will have to pay out the policies of their insured. If the country does not default, then insurers only collect the premiums paid by their clients for the right to have their bonds insured.

One other important aspect of bonds is that they may be issued in any currency. This is very important since currencies tend to fluctuate, that is, gain or lose value. If a country issues bonds, and that country's currency tanks, or loses significant value, then investors may just decide to dump the bonds for whatever they can get. This can cause a country to enter an economic meltdown.

Therefore, both countries and private corporations may choose to issue their bonds in currencies other than that of their home country. So, countries and corporations may choose to issue their bonds in US Dollars, Euros, Swiss Francs, or perhaps Yen. The important thing is that the currency is stable and accepted by investors around the world. If a bond is issued in a currency that is not trusted by investors, the bond would essentially be worthless.

Corporate bonds function the same way as sovereign bonds. These bonds are a means for companies to obtain financing through other means that isn't through the issuance of stock. Corporate bonds are underwritten by reputable financial intermediaries and are insured in the derivatives market. And just like sovereign bonds, the higher the risk, the higher the yield.

Categories of bonds

There are several different categories of bonds. That is, not all bonds are created equal.

In the previous section, we discussed two types of bonds: sovereign bonds and corporate bonds. They both function in the same manner and their yield is treated in the same way.

Now, let's have a closer look at the types of bonds out there:

- **Sovereign bonds**: As indicated in the previous section, there are bonds which are issued by sovereign nations. In the United States, they are called Treasury Bills or T-Bills. They are issued by the US Treasury and are bought by the intermediary banks through the Federal Reserve System. Most nations issue their bonds through their central banks.

- **Non-Sovereign bonds**: These types of bonds are usually issued for special purposes such as war bonds. They are a temporary means of raising capital and are usually linked to a very specific event such as a war. Countries may also issue these bonds to pay for expensive public works or to fund their currency.

- **High-quality corporate bonds**: We have already discussed corporate bonds. Yet, there are two types of corporate bonds — high and low quality. High-quality bonds are determined by a company's credit rating. This is done through a ratings agency such as Fitch, Standard and Poor's or Moody's. These are solid companies with great track records, healthy finances and low risk of default. They have a lower yield since they have a lower risk.

- **Low-quality bonds**: These are the so-called "junk bonds." These are bonds that are issued by corporations with not-so-good track records and may even represent a risk of default. These corporations offer little in the way of interest, but if they do pay up, the yield may become very attractive. This is an example of a high-risk, high-reward situation. Junk bonds are excessively risk and if several firms default at the same time, may cause massive losses in the bond market.

• **Municipal bonds**: Local governments issue these. In the United States, individual states and cities may issues bonds. This is not always possible in other countries. So, it's up to each country's individual governance.

• **Mortgage-backed bonds**: These types of bonds are actively traded in the derivatives market. These bonds consist in mortgage lenders issuing bonds in order to obtain funding for the sole purpose of lending money to homebuyers in order to finance the purchase of their homes. In essence, these bonds are what funds home purchases. When they are sold, other institutions become the owners of the mortgages that are attached to those bonds. These are some of the most-favored investments by hedge funds.

• **Debt-collateralized bonds**: These are high-risk bonds as they are issued by lenders who are looking to fund the issuance of credit to customers. These credits could come in the way of loans, credit cards or car loans. These loans have a high-risk of default but do offer the best returns to investors.

Options Trading

Options trading is part of the derivatives market. An option, as its name suggests, gives a person the option to buy, or sell, shares, but does not create an obligation. It is a derivative since it is valued on an underlying asset, in this case, stock.

Options are issued when there is speculation about a stock price. Essentially, the shareholder may choose to sell at a given price as specified in the contract but is not ultimately obligated to do so. The same goes for a buyer. What an option does is lock in a buy/sell price on that asset.

There are two parts to an options contract: the "put" and "call." A put option consists in granting someone the right to sell the underlying asset. When that happens, the parties involved in the contract agree on the price and terms of the sale.

A call option grants someone the right to buy the underlying asset in question. By this logic, if the buyer chooses to purchase the asset, the buyer will do so at the price and terms indicated in the contract.

The advantage of options is that it enables parties to agree on price and terms before actually engaging in the deal. Trades done outside options are subject to market forces. Therefore, buyers and seller may end up losing out on good deals.

Furthermore, options may lock in a price, similar to a futures contract, though a futures contract is tied to a commodity, such as oil, as the underlying asset whereas options have equities or even bonds, as the underlying asset.

FOREX

Foreign Exchange (FOREX) is a highly speculative market in which two, or more currencies, are pitted against each other. This market consists of buying and selling currencies based on their market value. It is a highly liquid market since investors are dealing specifically in money.

Equity or bond markets are not a liquid as FOREX since investors own paper assets which may, or may not, have enough funding to back their trades. This may result in a margin call thus leaving investors' positions unprotected. The end result could be an investor defaulting and needing to dump equities or securities in the market, at any price, in order to obtain cash.

As such, FOREX enables investors to trade in highly liquid assets denominated in currencies. There are FOREX ETFs which are essentially guaranteed to pay out since the underlying asset is cold, hard cash. Investors cannot enter the FOREX market unless they have the actual cash to do so.

FOREX looks at the exchange rates between two currencies. In essence, these could be two currencies of any two countries in the world. So, the combinations are virtually endless. It is also highly speculative because investors are betting against an appreciation or depreciation of one currency versus another.

For example, a trader buys 10,000 Euros at an exchange rate of 1EUR:1.18USD. That means that the investor would need 11,800 USD in order to purchase the 10,000 EUR. If the exchange rate changes from 1EUR:1.18USD to 1EUR:1.25USD, then the trader now has 12,500USD. He has made a profit of $700.

Performance indicators

Like anything in life, financial markets have indicators. These indicators may vary for international markets. But for the US markets, there are several indicators which investors can track in order to determine market trends.

We have already mentioned the Dow Jones, Nasdaq and S&P 500. These indices serve as an initial evaluation of stock market performance.

When the markets are doing well, they are said to be a "bull market." When the markets are performing badly, they are said to be a "bear market."

Here are some other statistical measures of market performance:

- **Advance/Decline Line**: This is a statistical model that tracks share prices. If overall stock prices are up, then the market is advancing. If overall share prices are down, then the market is declining.

- **10-day moving Average**: This tracks the same performance as the advance/decline line, but over a 10-day period. This provides a greater indication of short-term performance.

- **Economic indicators**: These indicators are not a specific result of stock performance but directly influence market performance. For example interest rates, consumer confidence index, consumer price index, housing prices, corporate earnings reports, and so on.

These performance indicators will enable investors to get a better idea of how the market is trending.

Impact on the average investor

When you hear that "the markets are down," there should be no cause for panic. It's quite normal for markets to fluctuate. The most important thing is to visualize market trends over weeks, months and years. If you have a short-term strategy, then looking at a six-month trend can help you gain a good perspective and where to go.

If you hear that "the markets are up," then you also need to track the moving average as getting into a market at the top may set you up for losses as the market may turn. Therefore, investors need to be keen on what market trends are and determine the best time to get in, or out, based on expectations on return.

The words thing an investor can do is ride out a market. Unless you have a long-term strategy, riding out a market will only set you up for significant losses.

Chapter 3: Investment Vehicles

In this chapter, we're going to be taking a closer look at investment vehicles. These investment vehicles are mainly issued by financial institutions in particular Banks.

In contrast to the stock market where equities, bonds and other types of securities are traded, the investment vehicles that we will discuss are issued by private banks. These banks issue certificates of deposit, mutual funds, or annuities which are backed by equities traded in the stock market.

The investment vehicles issued by private banks and other financial institutions are available to the average investor. Investing in these types of products requires a trip down to your local bank and a talk with your investment advisor. Investment advisors won't be able to provide you with insight on what the best available options would be for you.

The criteria that go into selecting an investment vehicle depends on the capital that the investor has available for investing, the expected returns on those investments, and the level of risk tolerance that the investor is willing to accept.

Based on that criteria, an average investor may negotiate one of the products that the bank has to offer them. The selection of these investment products will depend largely on the certainty of the product itself. For example, an investor might choose to invest in a shorter-term vehicle, and therefore, may choose a short-term investment such as a 30-day certificate of deposit.

On the other hand, if an investor is willing to put their money aside for a longer period of time, they may choose to take on a financial product and would go beyond the 30-day period. For instance, an investor might choose to set some money aside for a 180-day term or even for one year. A long-term investment strategy may be highlighted by the selection of long-term vehicles such as a long-term certificate of deposit.

In the previous chapter, we took a look at the stock market and focused on both the average investor and large institutional investors. In this particular discussion, we won't be looking at large institutional investors. Rather, we will be looking and the average investor and how they can set some money aside to put toward the investment products offered by a traditional Bank.

In this discussion, we're going to be considering the average retail bank that deals directly, one-on-one with customers and offers a range of products that go from savings and Loans to moderate investment products. We won't be considering large investment banks such as JPMorgan or Merrill Lynch.

It's worth noting that the money which investors will set aside toward investing in the products offered by retail banks will more than likely come from a portion of their earnings. These are surplus earning which have been saved. As such, the average investor will be more risk-averse as compared large institutional investors such as hedge funds.

As mentioned in the previous chapter, hedge funds are more willing to take on higher risk since they're seeking a higher return. Plus, the proportion of a higher risk, higher reward lead hedge funds toward seeking riskier investment vehicles. The average investor, who is more risk-averse, will be looking for safer investment instruments. Consequently, retail banks offer safer instruments for small investors to choose from. This not only enables investors to put their money to work, but it also allows a lower level of risk.

Certificates of Deposit

The first investment product that we will discuss is called a "certificate of deposit."

A certificate of deposit, as its name suggests, is a certificate issued with a specified face value. Its face value is agreed upon by both the bank and the investor. Most banks will offer a range of investments. For example, certificates of deposit will range from 1 to $1,000, $1,001 to 5000 and so on. There is no set range; this is up to each institution.

Whatever the bank chooses to offer to its customers depends on the investment strategies that both the investor and the bank are working to implement. Certificates of deposit are considered safer investments since they mature on a fixed date and at a specified rate. A certificate of deposit will have the backing of the issuing financial institution, and depending on that institution's credit rating, the certificate will be riskier or safer.

In general terms, an investor may not withdraw their investment prior to the maturity date. So, if a certificate of deposit has a 30-day term attached to it, the investor may not withdraw their money until the end of that 30-day term. If they choose to do so, the bank may stipulate that the investor must pay the penalty for early withdrawal.

Certificate of deposit offer a yield, that is an interest rate, which will be paid at the maturity of the certificate. This yield, or interest rate, is offered by the financial institution and agreed upon by the investor. It's important to note that the interest rate, or the yield, on certificates are set by prevailing market conditions. That is, whenever the interest rate that is set by the Federal Reserve and serves as a reference, will be the basis for the interest rate offered on the deposit. As a rule of thumb, shorter-term investments will have lower yield or interest rate. Longer-term investments will have a higher yield or higher interest rate.

Certificates of deposit have less inherent risk than other types of investment vehicles such as equities or stocks. Interest paid upon certificates will be lower than other riskier Investments. Much like bonds, there is an institution that is guaranteeing the payment of the certificate. For example, bonds issued by sovereign states are guaranteed to be paid by that state. So, unless a state may enter into default, the bond will be paid out.

The same goes for certificates of deposit. Unless the issuing financial institution is under risk of defaulting or going bankrupt, then it is virtually guaranteed that the certificate will be paid out what it matures.

One other important note: certificates of deposit are one of the ways in which banks finance their lending operations. The money collected from the issuance of certificates of deposit goes toward the issuance of loans and credit to other customers. One such type of certificates is called mortgage-backed certificates. Mortgage-backed certificates are specifically attached to mortgage loans. Investors who are willing to purchase these mortgage certificates can rest assured that their money is secured by the mortgages that other customers will acquire. Therefore, the interest that the bank collects, in addition to the capital lent, will be used to pay back investors who purchased the mortgage-backed certificates.

Mutual Funds

Another investment product offered by banks and financial investment institutions are mutual funds.

In short, mutual funds are a pool of money that is collected from various investors. Banks then invest this pool of funds. The funds the go toward investing in securities, for example, stocks, bonds, and other financial assets.

Since mutual funds are invested in the stock market, they are managed by professional money managers. These managers will allocate the funds into a basket of securities. For example, mutual funds may be invested in commodities such as oil and natural gas. Other types of mutual funds may go fully into stocks.

The investment strategy that money managers implement may vary according to the philosophy of each fund. If investors wish to get a higher return on a mutual fund, they may agree to have the fund invested in higher-risk securities. These higher risk securities may include corporate bonds which may be issued by companies in a riskier financial position. Nevertheless, they may offer a higher rate of return.

Other investment strategies may seek to find a more diversified approach. This diversified approach may be highlighted by investing in stocks, commodities, and bonds. Diversified mutual funds offer a better yield a reduced risk since the fund's performance does not depend on a single underlying asset. In fact, a diversified mutual fund spreads out risk and offsets potential losses of one asset with the gains from another

In general terms, mutual funds are made up by hundreds of different stocks. Therefore, mutual funds are typically diversified even if they are fully invested in stocks. Nevertheless, mutual funds will include bonds, among other securities, as a means of offsetting any potential losses from the stocks themselves.

In essence, mutual funds are like a small company. This company will take the money from investors and put it to work in the stock market. In many ways, it is similar to a hedge fund.

As noted earlier, a hedge fund is a club that takes money from investors, or members of the club, and invests that money as a pool. Mutual funds work in much the same way. Mutual funds tend to be much more conservative than hedge funds.

Thus, when the average investor buys into a mutual fund, they are actually buying a share of ownership into the mutual fund corporation. So, when the mutual fund corporation purchases shares of a company such as Facebook, the average investor is not really purchasing ownership of Facebook. Since the investor has purchased a share of ownership into the mutual fund company, that investor is actually the owner of the mutual fund company and not the stocks of the companies in which the mutual fund has invested.

There are different types of mutual funds.

The first kind is called the "fixed-income mutual fund." A fixed-income mutual fund is a type that is invested in bonds such as government or corporate bonds. Since bonds have a set yield, they offer a fixed income. Therefore, there is an expected rate of return that investors can count on when purchasing into this kind of mutual fund.

Another type of mutual fund is called an "index fund." These funds are generally attached to one of the major stock indices. For example, funds such as these may be pegged to the Dow Jones, NASDAQ or S&P 500. The return on these types of funds solely depends on market performance. So, if the market is booming, then investors can expect a higher rate of return. On the other hand, if markets are down, investors can expect a lower rate of return or even a potential loss.

Another type of mutual fund is called a "balanced fund." As I stated earlier, this is the type of fund that chooses to have a balanced approach between stocks and bonds. A balanced fund offers a diversified investment strategy which investors should consider to be safe.

One final note is that mutual funds have fees attached to them. These fees are charged for the administration of the fund. There is an annual fee which is charged for the operation of the fund. This can range from 1 to 3% of the fund's value. In addition, there may be other fees that come in the form of commissions. These commissions are paid upfront when investors purchase the fund. In short, this is the way mutual fund companies make money from running the fund itself. In addition, they will make money from the performance of the fund.

Annuities

Annuities are another type of investment offered by banks or insurance companies. They are often misunderstood since they tend to be complex in their calculation. Basically, annuities are a type of insurance which the average investor will pay a monthly or annual fee, and at the maturity of the term, the investor will receive a lump sum of money typically paid out monthly.

Just like any other insurance, the amount of money that the annuity will pay out will depend on the premium paid by the customer. Moreover, if a customer pays a larger premium, they will receive a larger payout. Depending on the annuity's term, the investor may choose to receive a lump-sum payment at the maturity of the fund or receive the fixed monthly payment.

Annuities are a typical investment made with retirement in mind. When an individual decides to purchase an annuity, they are thinking about contributing a specific amount of money, for example, every month, with the intent of guaranteeing their income in their retirement years.

One specific drawback of annuities is that the payments will last for a specific amount of time. So, depending on the terms of the annuity, payments may be made for, for say, 20 years. This means that the annuitant will be guaranteed an annual payment broken down into monthly payments for 20 years. Therefore, there is a risk that's the annuitant may outlive the number of payments agreed upon.

Another drawback of annuities is that they tend to be illiquid. The money that is deposited into an annuity may not be withdrawn until after an amount of time as specified in the terms of the annuity. This ensures that the annuity will not be insolvent, that is, will run out of money to pay all of the other investors who bought into the annuity fund.

In general terms, annuities are sold by insurance companies. This is why they function much the same way traditional insurance does. For example, life insurance is a pool of money collected by all of the customers who pay the premiums toward their life insurance policies. When a person passes, money is withdrawn from that fund, and the policy is paid out. Consequently, annuities work in the same manner.

Annuities are a great supplement to Social Security payments. In addition, it is recommended that individuals consider purchasing an annuity when they don't expect to collect social security. This is a way of putting money aside for retirement years when individuals will depend on a fixed income.

Portfolios

Investment portfolios are a collection of the different types of financial assets that an investor holds in their possession. This collection of assets can range from traditional equities such as stocks and bonds to other types of investments such as commodities, annuities or cash deposited in traditional bank accounts.

Wealthier individuals may seek professional advice from money managers who will help them allocate their assets in such a way that they generate the highest possible return. The allocation of assets largely depends on the investment strategy selected. An investor who is more inclined to a short-term, high-profit strategy will choose to allocate their assets in higher return instruments and thereby expose themselves to a higher level of risk. On the other hand, investors with a long-term strategy may seek to invest in safer investment vehicles such as bonds or annuities.

An important point to consider is the need to diversify. An investment portfolio comprised solely of one type of asset supposes a higher level of risk. For instance, a portfolio invested solely in equities such as stocks would represent 100% exposure to the stock market. Therefore, fluctuations in the market may represent considerable losses, or gains, for that particular portfolio.

A diversified, or balanced approach, will enable investors to make sure that any potential losses may be offset by the gains produced by other assets in the portfolio. This is why it is very important that the average investor become familiar with the contents of their portfolio. In addition, tracking the performance of a portfolio is vital to protecting investments against potential market shocks.

This doesn't mean that tracking portfolio should be a full-time job, but it does mean that an investor should be well aware of where their assets and how they are allocated.

Chapter 4: Day Trading

Throughout this book, we have discussed how investors may seek investment opportunities in different financial markets. We have discussed stocks, bonds, mutual funds, commodities, and even derivatives.

In order for most investors to enter financial markets, they must hire a broker to buy and sell financial assets on their behalf. In order to do this, brokers must be officially licensed to do so. Furthermore, they work for financial institutions that are duly registered and supervised by official government regulatory bodies.

However, an average individual may choose to enter financial markets on their own. This can be done through a brokerage company that offers average investors the opportunity to manage their own portfolio.

Individual investors who seek to enter financial markets may do so by using online platforms offered by traditional brokerage companies. All an individual needs to do is open, and fund, an account and learn how to use the platform. This will enable an individual to become a trader.

One such type of trader is called a day trader. Day traders are individuals who open their position at the beginning of the trading day and generally close their positions at the end of the trading day. This open and close generally corresponds to the opening and closing of a major stock exchange. For example, a trader may choose to follow the opening and closing of the New York Stock Exchange.

Some individuals have made day trading a full-time job. The reason for this is because they are able to make enough money to cover their expenses and fund their lifestyle. However, being a day trader is a highly speculative endeavor. A day trader must be keenly aware of the investment vehicles that they are purchasing when to purchase them, and most importantly, when to sell them. It's important to note that being a day trader requires knowledge, not only in the functioning of financial markets themselves but also in the investment platforms and tools available to them.

In this chapter, we will take an in-depth look at what it takes to become a day trader. But before we get into the specifics of becoming a trader, it is important to point out that this type of activity is not for everyone. Those individuals who become full-time day traders must ultimately give up their jobs in order to dedicate the time and attention needed to trade on a daily.

In addition, being a day trader is not a steady source of income. Just as it is possible to make large sums of money on great deals, it is also possible to lose a considerable sum of money. Thus, day trading is not the type of activity where you can put all your eggs in one basket. Done right, day trading can become a very lucrative activity.

So, if you've made it to this point in this book, it is because you are serious about engaging in the trade of financial assets. So, let's take a closer look at what it takes to become a day trader.

How to become an investor

The first rule to becoming an investor is having money to invest. That means individuals who seek to become investors must have some extra cash set aside for this purpose. For those individuals who live paycheck-to-paycheck, investing may not be feasible since all of their income goes toward funding their lifestyle and have very little in the way of savings.

Now, it is worth noting that it is not necessary to have millions of dollars in order to become an investor. Most financial institutions will require a minimum investment of around $500 for investing online.

The second rule to consider when becoming an investor is setting an investment strategy. The expectations of investors define investment strategies. That is, what an investor seeks to gain out of investing their money into a given financial market. If an investor is looking to get rich quick, they may choose to find high-yield investments. Of course, we have discussed how high-yield Investments also come with a high level of risk.

What the average investor seeks by putting their money to work is to generate alternative sources of income. These alternative sources of income are those that do not depend on having a job. While jobs may offer a steady paycheck every month, the potential for salary growth is rather limited. For an employee to receive an increase in their salary, certain conditions must be met. Generally, a raise is associated with a promotion or switching to another higher-paying job

Day trading may potentially lead to a situation where an investor may generate enough passive income whereby the investor will not be required to work in order to fund and maintain their lifestyle. What most investors look for in an investment strategy is being able to achieve financial security and financial freedom. This is the core tenet of becoming an investor.

Let's compare being an employee, and having a steady paycheck, to becoming an investor and having a steady stream of income as a result of investing in financial instruments.

After a certain amount of years, employees may collect a pension and/or social security. These payouts typically come after decades of work and will ensure income for an individual during their retirement years, that is, when they can no longer work. Pensions and social security are limited, and their growth potential is virtually nil. Moreover, more pensions and social security payments may not be inherited to future generations

On the other hand, savvy investing may lead to unlimited growth potential of income. Unlimited growth potential is due to the fact that wise investing is not capped off at any point. As a matter of fact, profitable Investments will not only produce income for an unlimited amount of time, but they also increase in the income generated. One such example may be a mutual fund that gains in value over time.

Other Financial assets with unlimited growth potential are stocks. For instance, if an investor owns a given amount of shares in a company whose valuation skyrockets due to their performance, this investor may choose to sell and clean up thanks to the exponential growth in that company's valuation.

The next rule to becoming an investor is related to mindset. Becoming an investor depends largely on the tolerance of risk. For those folks who are risk-averse, there are many safe investment vehicles such as certificates of deposit or government bonds. However, becoming a day trader is a riskier proposition. Therefore, a more adventurous mindset is needed in order to become successful in trading. In many ways, becoming a successful investor means that you are not afraid to take on the risks that come with making money through investing in financial markets

How to purchase funds online

The emergence of the internet has allowed the average investor to take control of their own investment strategies. In the past, an investor needed to go through a broker in order to allocate their money into financial markets. The internet, however, now offers a myriad of opportunities for the average investor the sink their teeth into.

As such, investors can use the internet, through the use of online trading platforms, to buy and sell equities. Trading platforms are offered by many of the large brokerage firms that have invested time and money into developing these systems. Consequently, any individual with enough funds may choose to open an account in order to begin trading.

It is recommended to utilize a training platform in order to learn how to purchase financial assets. The reason for this is because an average individual may not be familiar with the mechanics of buying and selling stocks. However, the use of a training platform will familiarize new investors to the way stocks are traded. Thus, the use of a trading platform cuts out the need for a middleman.

This enables investors to take full control of the management of their fund. This is significant since stockbrokers and money managers will decide how to invest a customer's money. Needless to say, customers and brokers don't always see eye-to-eye with regard to investment strategy. Thus, being able to control investment strategies is an attractive quality of online trading platforms.

There are several trading platforms out there available for the average investor. In this book, we are not endorsing any particular trading platforms. But we are advocating the use of trading platforms in order to buy and sell financial assets. It is recommended that the average investor look into all the possible platforms out there so that they may choose the one that best suits their needs

Of course, not all platforms are created equal. Some platforms offer a lower minimum amount to fund the account but may charge higher trading fees. Other platforms may have a higher buy-in but charge lower transaction fees.

Another important aspect to consider when choosing a platform is the support that comes with that specific platform. Some financial institutions offer access to their analytics and data so that account holders may see what human stock brokers are looking at and make investment decisions accordingly.

An interesting quality of online trading is that brokerage firms offer free test accounts with their platforms. These platforms offer the real experience but do not require a monetary deposit. The investor is given virtual money to invest in the platform and make trading decisions accordingly. The results obtained from the transactions made in the free test account are indicative of the outcomes that real trades would have produced.

One very important word of caution here is to beware of transaction fees. Transaction fees are generally charged per trade. A brokerage firm may choose to charge a flat rate of $5 for trade every time an investor chooses to buy or sell. This implies that there will automatically be a $5 transaction fee attached to all trades. This is very important to take into consideration because transaction fees add up and could potentially derail the profits made on a trade.

How to purchase a tracker fund

Tracker funds are basically the same as an average ETF. Tracker funds are essentially an index fund, such as a mutual fund, and can be indexed to virtually any market in the world. In essence, the success of the fund will depend on the performance of the index that it is tracking. For example, a tracker fund that is indexed to the S&P 500 will yield a profit if the S&P 500 makes produces good results. Conversely, if the S&P 500's performance is poor, then the tracker fund may lose money.

The purpose of purchasing a tracker fund is to gain exposure to a broader base. So instead of limiting exposure to a certain group of stocks or companies, tracker funds allow investors to gain exposure to the entire Market. Therefore, the performance of the market is not solely dependent on a handful of companies. Rather, it is a measure of the entire market's performance.

Since a tracker fund is essentially an ETF, investors do not actually own any shares of any company. The actual owner of the equities is the financial institution that is selling the tracker fund. Therefore, tracker funds, or index funds, are another form of paper asset.

Tracker funds are also a form of passive investing. Since the fund is made out of a broad segment of the market, there is no individual trading of individual stocks. So, investors who purchase the fund may sit back and track the market's performance. Since the fund is dependent on market performance, there is no specific yield attached to the fund.

Index funds are also a great way of low-cost investing while gaining significant exposure to the markets. A good indicator of how well a market is performing is the market's performance over time. For instance, if a market has produced annual returns of 5% over the last 10 years, it can be expected that an index fund will produce a yield of approximately 5%. If the index fund is purchased during a bull market, that is, a market in expansion, the returns may be expected to be greater. However, if the market is down, or bearish, then returns on the fund could be expected to be lower.

One other important consideration with regard to tracker funds is that risk tends to be lower since exposure to the entire market dilutes the possibility of risk. Subsequently, index funds provide a solid investment vehicle that can produce results based on market averages while limiting risk to acceptable levels.

It is also important to consider that there are costs and fees attached to the purchase and sale of these funds. This is why it is important for investors to do their research and find out what fees are attached to these funds.

Investment platforms

As discussed earlier, not all investment platforms are created equal.

While all platforms tend to have the same characteristics, not all of them have the same transaction fees attached to them. Also, it is important to consider the availability of financial assets which can be traded on a given platform.

Thus, it is highly recommended that investors look into discount brokers who offer online investment services. These discount brokers may offer trades as low as $2 per trade. However, it is also important to find out if there are any management, or maintenance, fees attached in addition to transaction fees.

If you choose to get into FOREX trading, then it would be highly recommended to seek a platform specially dedicated to FOREX. In addition, if you are looking to invest in markets outside of the United States, then you will need to search for a platform with those capabilities.

Since I am not endorsing any specific platforms, it is vital to do research into any platform you might consider working with. Personally, I would not sign up to any trading platform that does not offer me a free practice account.

A free practice account is crucial since it will give you a sense of how the platform works before you actually risk any real money. If you can produce good results on a practice account, then you can feel confident you will actually make money on the real thing. However, practice accounts usually have limited functionality such as a short trial period. So, it is important to make the most of it while you can.

Another important aspect to consider is the type of support provided for that platform. If a given platform offers little support, then you can be sure that if you run into trouble, you will be on your own. This is one of the dangers that come with discount brokerage firms. So, if support is important to you, then you may have to dish out a few extra dollars in terms of maintenance fees in order to get support.

A good rule of thumb is to do a thorough search on the opinions of real customers on the use of a platform you are interested in. Also, you may choose to visit that firm's offices and get information from an actual human being. If you are able to connect with other investors, word of mouth reference may end up being a lifesaver.

How to determine when to buy

Determining when to buy a stock or investment vehicle is as much an art as it is science. So far, there hasn't been any single investor out there who has managed to perfect a system that can determine the right time to buy a stock or equity.

So, how can you tell when the best time to purchase the stock Equity would be?

The answer to this question depends on how closely you follow the markets. If you are willing to invest the time needed in order to follow market trends and gain a clear picture of where individual stocks are going, you can get a good idea of when to buy a based on the trend of that stock. For example, if a company is trading in a range of $100 to $110, anything in that range would be considered normal.

However, if that particular stock happened to follow below $100, and you know that this is well below its usual market price, then you can safely assume that it is time to buy. Of course, you need to understand why the stock fell below its floor, that is, the $100 price. If it's due to market forces, then you can buy on the dip. However, if the drop in the price of a stock is due to poor earnings, or problems within the firm, then it might not be the best time to purchase that stock. In fact, buying stock of a troubled company may end up costing you more money in the long run.

That is why day traders live and die by the analytics and information they have access to. You can purchase premium subscription services to financial information sources which will provide you with analytics and insights into the trends of markets, individual stocks and other investment vehicles.

Furthermore, you need to be careful not to buy when the market is at an all-time high. For example, if a market is breaking records, then you need to be very careful in which stocks you will invest. The reason for this is that when you buy at the top, there's no place to go but down. Similarly, if you buy at the bottom, there's no place to go but up. However, determining where that bottom is, is as hard to predict as the weather.

Knowing when to buy a stock, or equity also depends on your gut. You need to do research and put effort into knowing where market trends are going. But at the end of the day, there's a component of intuition that will tell you when the right time to buy is. This intuition is honed through experience and understanding of markets.

Another word of caution: be wary of those pundits on television who claim to have Insider information and are telling you when to buy and when to sell. Ultimately, these so-called experts are human and could be wrong. That is why it is important to take any financial advice you hear with a grain of salt as I've always said, trust but verify. That way, you can make an informed decision as to whether to buy and wait until the price drops further.

How to determine when to sell

Determining when to sell is just as hard as it to determine when to buy.

Knowing when to sell is an art form. Many investors make the mistake of waiting for the price to keep going up. When you understand the way investing works, you will know what a normal price for a stock or equity would be.

For instance, if a stock is trading in the range of $100 to $110, a price that is above $110 would be territory for you to consider selling. Suppose that that particular stock reaches 120. At that point, you must consider selling because if you hold, the price may come back down, and you would miss out on a good opportunity.

If you were playing a long-term strategy and you're not concerned with buying and selling every time the price goes up or down, then minor market fluctuations should not concern you. However, if you have a short-term trading strategy, then you need to sell as soon as the price goes beyond a range you have determined to be normal.

You may also hear the term "bubble." A bubble consists of investor behavior whereby they pay increasingly large amounts for a particular stock or equity. You can easily identify a bubble when prices are far higher than you have observed in the past. For example, if the stock is trading at $100, but it has progressively climbed 200, then you might consider that to be bubble territory, at which point, you must sell immediately. If you choose to hold on to the stock in hopes of making an even larger profit, you may set yourself up for greater disappointment when the price comes down, and you sell at a lower profit.

This is why knowing when to sell hinges on your mindset. Overly ambitious investors will commit the cardinal sin of holding onto stocks for too long. In a way, it's better to be a day early than a day late. I would always recommend selling at any time you are making a profit. By waiting too long, you may end up potentially taking a loss simply because you tried to time the market

Timing the market is incredibly difficult because no one knows what the top of that market might be. Financial markets are highly volatile and unpredictable. Therefore, your common sense, intuition, and experience will tell you when the right time to sell will be. If you happen to sell too soon, don't worry; there will always be more opportunities to buy solid equities at low prices.

One other important piece of advice is to avoid trying to hit a home run. Most investors dream of cleaning up in one deal. Many picture that making one deal will solve all their problems for the rest of their lives. Well those deals are out there, and they do exist, but the likelihood of making such a deal is very low. So, never regret selling as long as you make money. You can regret a sale when you lose money.

Chapter 5: The Language of Investing

In this chapter, we'll be taking a look at three important elements that make up any successful investment strategy. So far, we have discussed a great deal of information pertaining to the mechanics of investing. However, the time has come to focus more on strategy and the crucial elements that can make or break a successful investment strategy.

Often, investors lose sight of these important elements, the first of which is diversification. Diversification is a crucial factor in mitigating risk.

Also, risk management is a fundamental part of successful portfolio management. When investors don't understand risk or engage in high-risk trading, they expose themselves to potentially losing a fair bit, if not, their entire Investments.

In addition, investors' expectations play a pivotal role in the decisions they make into the investment strategy that is implemented. One measure of these expectations is the annual return on investments. As such, investors expect to earn a specific amount of money derived from their Investments.

But it is one thing to manage expectations, and it's another to deal with an actual return on. Consequently, investor expectations are contrasted by actual returns, and the difference will determine if an investment strategy has been successful or not.

This is what we call the "language of investing." And by understanding this language, you can improve your chances of becoming a successful investor. By understanding this language, you can set yourself up for success.

The importance of diversification

Diversification is an overarching theme in investing. You will hear investors talk about this term when planning their investment strategies.

But what is diversification?

Well, diversification consists in, literally, not putting all your eggs in one basket. Diversification is about spreading your investable assets across different types of Investments.

Let's consider the opposite of diversification first.

Consider an investor who has $100 earmarked for investing in the stock market. This investor chooses to put his full $100 into shares of one corporation. If that corporation is a solid company and is making money, then the chances of making money on this $100 investment will be good. However, if for some reason, the company runs into trouble and posts negative earnings reports, then the chances of losing money maybe high.

In this example, the investor is exposed to a high level of risk since investing in one financial asset means that your chances of making, or losing, money hinge on the performance of that one particular asset.

As such, diversification is about mitigating and reducing risk. When you spread your eggs out into different baskets, you're protecting yourself by determining what investments will have the best chances of making money and potentially offsetting the losses that other Investments may incur.

Let's see this diversification strategy.

The investor who has $100 earmarked for investing, chooses to break that $100 investment into four parts. That means the $25 will be allotted to each type of investment. The first $25 will go into the stock market through the purchase of equities. The next $25 will go toward the purchase of mutual funds. The next $25 will be allocated to the purchase of bonds. And the last $25 will be invested in a certificate of deposit.

As you can see, this diversification strategy looks to offset the potential losses of one asset class over the other. Let's assume that the stock market goes down. Since stocks are down, that $25 investment may now be $20. However, the performance of the mutual funds is higher since that particular fund has been indexed to a different market. The initial $25 investment is now $30. In this example, the gains of one market have offset the losses of the other. As such, this investor broke even.

Therefore, diversification is crucial to ensuring the success of any investment portfolio. One clear example of this are index funds. As discussed earlier, index funds offer investors exposure to an entire market or a considerable segment of one. Consequently, the performance of an index fund hinges on the performance of the entire market. So, if one individual stock is underperforming, the remaining stocks can pick up the slack and offset the losses of one underperforming stock.

This example of diversification offers investors a safety net. While it's true that there are always risks in any type of investment, diversification serves to reduce that level of risk down to more manageable levels.

One other key advantage of diversification is that diversification enables a portfolio to be broken up into different pieces. Our previous example highlighted how a portfolio could be broken up into four parts. So, if one part is underperforming, the investor can choose to get rid of that particular component and allocate those funds into better-performing assets. This would be virtually impossible under an investment strategy that is focused solely on one asset class, or one individual stock.

Annual return on investments

The best measure of success of an investment is what is known as "annual return on investments." Stated earlier, annual return on investment begins with investor expectations. That is, what investors expect to gain when allocating resources toward an investment. For example, an investor who sets aside $100 into a given investment will expect to gain a specific amount at the end of one year. Hence, the term annual rate of return.

However, it is important to track the real performance of an investment by determining the gain or loss of that investment.

Let's assume the following:

An investor that allocated $100 toward the purchase of an individual stock is expecting to earn a 10% return at the end of one year. This expectation is based on that stocks' previous performance and market trends. Thus, the investor expects to get $110 at the end of one year. This is known as the expected rate of return.

Throughout the year, the stock's performance has been tracked. At the end of the year, the stock produced a 10% return. This means that the investors' expectations were on par with the actual performance of the stock. Let's assume now the same stock, at the end of one year, produced a 7% return. That means investors' expectations were not met. Conversely, that same stock produced an 11% return meaning that investors' expectations were exceeded.

This example underscores the importance of managing both expectation and reality. When investors have unrealistic expectations, they may choose to engage in riskier investment practice. This is true of hedge funds playing the derivatives market.

In the derivatives market, there is ample room for making significant gains that outperform traditional market returns. For an individual investor, expected returns may be linked to the market average. For instance, if a given market has produced, on average, a return of 5% a year over the last decade, then it would be safe to assume that a 5% return would be likely.

Also, Risk plays an important factor. If an investor is looking to reduce risk, they may accept a lower rate of return on a given investment. It is important to highlight at this point that the rate of return is nothing more than the money you expect to make from the investment.

To calculate return on investment, the following formula may be utilized:

ROI = (Gain from Investment – Cost of Investment) / Cost of Investment

As you can see, this formula contemplates the gain from an investment, that is, the increase in price of an investment minus the cost of the investment itself. This result is divided by the cost of the investment. The result is expressed in percentage terms. Therefore, the higher the percentage, the higher the return on the investment.

This formula does not take into account any specific time period. And while it is a simple way of calculating return on investment, the time period which it measures depends on data that is supplied to that formula.

Let's look at a practical example:

An investor chooses to invest $100 in shares of ABC company. After one month, this investor chooses to sell his shares of ABC company. The sale price was $110. On the surface, it is easy to see that the investor has gained $10.

Now, let's apply the formula that we looked at earlier.

ROI = (110 − 100) / 100 = 0.1 or 10%

The results from the calculation of this formula show how this investor gained 10% in a one-month period. Moreover, this calculation could be done over a one-year period. So, this calculation can be done over any length of time so long as the data reflects that amount of time.

Calculation of return on investment allows investors to determine if their investment is profitable and if such investments meet their expected returns.

The results produced by the calculation of return on investment allow investors to determine if allocating their money into a given investment vehicle is worth their while or if they would be better suited investing their money elsewhere.

One other note: not all Investments have the same yield. Some Investments produce higher yields than others. Therefore, the return on investment reflects the risk aversion attitude that investors may have. Also, it is a reflection of investors' investment strategy.

Risk Management

Risk management is a crucial factor that needs to be considered as a part of any solid investment strategy.

Throughout this book, we have discussed the importance of understanding risk and taking the necessary precautions to manage it effectively. When investors are clear on the importance of risk management, they're able to take effective steps in order to make sure that their Investments are protected.

Furthermore, decisions regarding the allocation of investments are deeply rooted in the implicit risk of that investment vehicle. For investors who are more risk-averse, they will seek to invest in financial instruments that are considered safer. These in instruments include government bonds, certificates of deposit, high-quality corporate bonds or more conservative mutual funds.

Institutional investors such as hedge funds, generally seek higher returns on their Investments. As such, these institutional investors are more prone to take on higher levels of risk. Moreover, they are the first to collect when payments are due on those investments.

For the average day trader, risk as a fundamental part of understanding which equities to purchase. Day traders who have a conservative long-term investment strategy may choose to purchase equities of renowned companies which have a solid track record. These companies will not only pay a healthy dividend but will also reduce the likelihood of potential default or bankruptcy.

It is very important that day traders, or average investors, understand the importance of a more balanced approach. As noted in the section on diversification, a balanced approach enables to spread out risk over different asset classes and investment vehicles. Consequently, diversification is the antidote for investors to counteract inherent risks in any investment they choose to make.

Also, we have noted that higher risk implies a higher return. This is why institutional investors, like hedge funds or large investment banks, will choose to take on higher risk in order to maximize their potential returns. An average investor should be wary of engaging in risky trading since a bad deal could represent significant losses to their portfolio.

In addition, a portfolio that is laden with high-risk Investments may lead to a potentially catastrophic loss when a market downturn wipes out any potential gains. This may even incur in losses. In Hollywood movies, it's common to see how stock traders gamble with their investors' money on high-risk, high-reward Investments only to lose all of their money in a swift market downturn. While it is true that being successful in a venture such as this can turn ordinary citizens into millionaires overnight, the fact of the matter is that the risk far outweighs any potential gains.

Risk can be quantified through the use of statistical models. These models require large amounts of data sets in order to feed them and produce a relatively accurate prediction of where the risk lies in a particular investment. The average investor, who trades on an online platform, may have access to the statistical models which can provide information on the potential risk of an investment.

So, some general guidelines to follow about investments are as follows

- focus on historical trends of those types of Investments
- seek professional advice if you are unsure about whether an investment is potentially risky
- avoid investing in instruments, or financial assets, which you know nothing or very little about
- beware of fads. When you see that a large number of investors flocking to a particular investment vehicle perhaps it might be time to stay away from it.

Ultimately, experience, common sense, and intuition will tell you if the risk that you are taking on in an investment will pay off in the end. It's important to note that you will never be free of risk. There is always risks in any type of investment out there. So, if an investment offers higher-than-usual returns, you must do your homework and make sure that you're not setting yourself up for significant losses down the road.

Chapter 6: Starting from Scratch: How to Grow Like the Pros

All good investors need motivation.

Often, investors are driven by the need to make a living. It is true that Hollywood tends to portray investors as greedy individuals whose sole purpose of investing is to make as much money as possible. Well, that may be true, the average investor, whether big or small, is driven by a fundamental human need to make a living for themselves.

Of course, everyone dreams of becoming rich one day particularly if this can be done without resorting to extreme efforts. Also, some individuals seek to get rich quick. History has proven that getting rich quick is as difficult as swimming across the Atlantic Ocean. That is, it is not completely out of the question, but it is extremely difficult.

In this chapter, we're going to be taking a look at some of the most famous investors in history. We'll take a look at their personal experiences and how they became rich as successful investors. From their stories, we will distill some of the most important lessons on investing.

It's worth noting that any investor who is just starting out should take a look at successful investors from the past and learn from their personal success stories. Considering that each individual is different, the point here is not to copy or mimic the actions taken by others.

The decisions made in the past were based upon the circumstances of that time. The present now has a different set of circumstances that may motivate different decisions. Nevertheless, there are general principles and lessons which are valid throughout any period in history

Through these lessons learned, new or inexperienced investors can gain a much broader understanding of what it takes to become a successful investor. The people who we will be discussing in this chapter have essentially made it rich.

Does that mean that this should be the ultimate goal of every investor?

Not necessarily. Every investor should first determine why they are even getting into investing in the first place. This will enable the development of an investment strategy. Once an investor has found their investment strategy, it becomes a lot easier to make decisions based on that investment philosophy. So, the investors featured in this chapter were folks who started off with virtually nothing and made their way up through the ranks. Their stories are meant to inspire and motivate the average investor by understanding that anything is possible.

One word of caution though: it's dangerous to compare yourself, as an investor to the big-league investors such as Warren Buffett. The danger here lies in the fact that many of these professional investors have been at this game for a very long time. They have gone through ups and downs, have had many losses, and have rebounded. Their main characteristic has been the focus and drive to stay in the market and perfect their skills.

Consequently, it is recommended that you avoid comparing yourself to other investors since each, individual investors' circumstances are different. While learning from successful investors is a significant way to develop your own investment skills, having a clear investment strategy will allow you to visualize the road map on which you have decided to travel. By keeping an eye on this road map, you will avoid the temptation of engaging in risky behaviors that may jeopardize your overall investment portfolio.

Warren Buffet

The first investor we're going to be looking at is Warren Buffett.

Warren Buffett is arguably the most famous and legendary investor in history. His holding company, Berkshire Hathaway, manages billions and billions of dollars in assets. These assets include equities bonds, private corporations, and cash Investments.

Warren Buffett wasn't born rich. In fact, he was just an average kid growing up who had a good head for business. From an early age, he was keen on building businesses and investing his money. He was known to be a very prudent teenager. The money he earned from summer jobs and after-school chores, would be put aside in a savings account. He believed that if he saved his money, he would not only have enough for a rainy day, but he would be able to invest that money into building his own business.

Buffet recalls being inspired by a book written by Benjamin Graham known as "The Intelligent Investor." This book not only inspired Buffett to become an investor but it also provided him with the general guidelines for becoming a successful investor.

Benjamin Graham, in his own right, is considered to be one of the most successful investors in history. However, his time was completely different to Warren Buffett's. Warren Buffett grew up in Omaha, Nebraska in the 1940s. Benjamin Graham had to become a successful investor in the 1920s and 30s. Nevertheless, the investment principles espoused by Graham enabled Warren Buffett to derive his own set of principles and guidelines which marked his investment strategy throughout his career.

Today, Warren Buffett is consistently in the top five of the richest people in the world. If you look closer at Warren Buffett's biography, you will notice that he is hardly a flashy and flamboyant person. In fact, he has always been a poster child for prudence and frugality. He is not the type of business person who you will see riding around in fancy cars and living in opulent mansions.

Warren Buffett's investment strategies have always focused on incremental growth. This implies that investors should not seek to find a magic bullet. Magic bullets are just that: magic. Therefore, they do not represent a true sustainable investment strategy. Quite the contrary, Buffett espouses an investment strategy that is focused on small and incremental gains. Over time, these smaller, incremental gains will compel each other to form exponential growth.

Warren Buffett is also known for his appreciation of compound interest. In short, compound interest consists in taking a specified sum of money, depositing it into an investment and allowing the gains from those investments to add up over time. Compound interest highlights how small, incremental gains can lead to larger exponential growth.

Basically, compounding works in the following manner:

Let's consider a safe investment such as a certificate of deposit. If an investor chooses to deposit $100 into that certificate, at the maturity of the certificate, the investor will receive the $100 plus the interest paid on that certificate. At this point, the investor can choose to spend the money that was produced from the investment. Or, the investor may choose to redeposit the $100 plus the interest gained from that investment into a new certificate of deposit. The new certificate of deposit will now calculate its yield based on the $100 plus the interest on that investment. Over time, the amount invested will grow and grow through smaller increments until it reaches a point where it grows exponentially. Since the sum invested has grown considerably as compared to the initial investment, we can say that the investment has compounded.

As you can see, this is hardly the most exciting investment strategy. But it is a virtually guaranteed that investors will make money. However, this is a long-term investment strategy and may not be appealing to those who are looking to get rich quick.

Considering that Warren Buffett is one of the richest people in the world, he was onto something with his investment strategy. That is why playing it safe often pays off more in the long run then rolling the dice for a short-term gain.

Chris Gardner

Chris Gardner is another of the world's most famous investors. His claim to fame came from his autobiography which was turned into a Hollywood movie starring Will Smith. The success of this film titled "In Pursuit of Happiness," catapulted Chris Gardner into investment lore.

If there was ever a rags-to-riches story, this is it. If you are interested in learning more about Chris Gardner's journey from rags to riches, you may watch the Hollywood film which chronicles his journey.

For now, we will focus on how he became a wealthy individual.

After struggling through adversity, he obtained his brokerage license. He then became a stock trader at one of New York's largest brokerage firms. Initially, he invested with his clients' money. As he earned commissions derived from his successful dealings, he took some of his earnings and invested them in his own name. His success with his clients' money, and his own led him to achieve wealth in a similar fashion as Warren Buffett.

The success of Chris Gardner's investment strategy was based upon reinvesting his gains from Investments. So, He was able to resist the temptation of having a high-flying life as a result of his new-found wealth as a stock trader. In fact, he kept a low profile for many years while he accrued a significant amount of wealth.

His track record and reputation as a successful trader enabled him to start his own capital investment firm. Gardner, along with other business partners, built one of the largest, and most successful, New York investment firms.

Gardner eventually sold his participation in this investment firm and reinvested is proceedings into assets which now fund his lifestyle. He is now a motivational speaker focusing on how to triumph over adversity and become a successful investor.

The core of his investment strategy is based on living within your means. That is, no matter how much money you make, it is important to consider that having a high-flying lifestyle is not conducive to building long-term wealth. This is a common bond between Gardner and Buffett.

Therefore, investors who seek to build considerable wealth and financial freedom must understand that maintaining a balanced lifestyle, along with prudent Investments, will enable them to become wealthy and help them to achieve financial security and freedom.

One very important common link between Chris Gardiner and Warren Buffett is risk aversion. These two investors are known for playing it safe most of the time. While there are times when you need to be aggressive, it's important to understand that playing it safe will get you to the finish line just about every time.

Another important note about Chris Gardner: his biggest motivator was to provide his family with a good life. This underscores the importance of family and providing for future generations has on the attitudes of most investors. Therefore, it is crucial that any sustainable, long-term strategy consider a balanced approach in which risk is mitigated as much as possible.

Ken Langone

Ken Langone is a traditional, old-school investor. He is an American billionaire businessman and investor whose claim to fame is financing the founders of The Home Depot.

Just like Warren Buffett and Chris Gardner, Ken Langone's beginning are humble, to say the least. He did not inherit a vast fortune from his wealthy family. In fact, he is a success story on how an individual can work their way up through the ranks of the business world and achieve ultimate success.

Langone's early career started in Wall Street as a stock trader and financial consultant. His early endeavors were focused on developing new businesses. As such, his company invested in up and coming new businesses. These investments began to grow considerably as companies became successful.

In the 1970s, Langone would go on to invent what is now known as Venture Capital. Venture capital, or VC, is a term that is used to describe individual investors and institutions who fund new start-up companies.

As described in an earlier chapter, investors who acquire stakes in private firms during their initial, start-up phase can clean up when a private firm goes public during their IPO. This is how Ken Langone's legendary investment career took off. Among the successful businesses that his firm helped finance, The Home Depot stands out as the largest one.

In contrast to Warren Buffett and Chris Gardner, who struck it rich in the stock market, Ken Langone's career as a venture capitalist highlights the importance of having a vision when choosing the best investments out there. It is necessary that venture capitalists have the foresight, expertise, and insight to determine what startup businesses could grow and become successful companies.

Nevertheless, there is a common thread among Buffett, Gardner, and Langone. They all believe in having prudent investment behavior. This is very important for venture capitalists since investing in startup businesses poses a considerably higher risk than corporate bonds. There are no guarantees that a startup will even become profitable much less grow into a company that reaches the IPO phase.

Therefore, a great deal of restraint needs to be exercised in determining which startups to invest in. Some startups look fabulous on paper, but in reality, they lack the fundamentals that will allow them to become a successful business in practice. Other times, startups have good products or business ideas, but their founders may lack the management skills and business knowledge needed to transform a potentially successful product into a great business.

So, the moral of the story is that investors must keep a cool head whenever considering potential Investments.

Oprah Winfrey

Oprah Winfrey, who is best known as a television personality, is also a billionaire investor. She's one of the wealthiest women in the world and has proven how intelligent investment strategies can take an average individual and turn them into a billionaire.

Just like the previous investors, we have discussed in this chapter, Oprah Winfrey does not come from a wealthy family. In fact, she worked her way up through the ranks of television studios to the point where she was able to land her own daytime television show.

Most individuals would have been perfectly content by becoming a famous television personality and living off the income that comes with that status. Indeed, Oprah Winfrey made a good living for herself as a result of her talents and success on television.

Nevertheless, she highlights an important attitude that all investors must keep in mind: she was not content with the success she had achieved. In fact, she was looking to increase her investments, not out of greed, but out of a desire to achieve higher success.

Just like the previous investors discussed in this chapter, greed is not a motivating factor; rather it is success. All successful investors are driven by achieving success. Complacency is not in their vocabulary. And so, they seek to build upon past successes.

Oprah Winfrey is a good example of how Warren Buffett's prudent investment strategies prove highly successful. One such example is her investment in a company called Weight Watchers. In October of 2015, she invested $43 million into the purchase of stock valued at $7 a share. Eventually, Weight Watchers took off, and its share price went from $7 to $101. This meant that Oprah's initial investment of $43 million became $427 million.

This example underscores how understanding the value hidden away in an underperforming stock can lead to substantial gains. This is why investors must always do their homework and research new opportunities. If you look to get into a stock, or market, when everyone else is trying to get in, then you are most likely too late.

This buy-low, sell-high philosophy is one of the core tenets of all successful investors. The tricky part is being able to identify those investment opportunities. The most important factor that can help any investor achieve success in a venture such as this comes from experience and learning. This where every successful investor must take the time to put in the effort needed to master their craft. This will enable them to reach a point where they can learn to successfully identify potential investment opportunities.

Andrew Carnegie

The last investor we will be looking at in this chapter is Andrew Carnegie.

Andrew Carnegie was one of the wealthiest men in history. His claim to fame came during the Industrial Age in the United States. Just like the four previous investors we have discussed, he did not come from a wealthy family. In fact, he was the son of Scottish immigrants who came to America with nothing to their name.

He worked his way up through the business world and eventually made a name for himself in the steel industry. The steel industry was one of the industries which drove American economic expansion to a point where it became a global powerhouse. His Investments in developing the steel industry allowed him to amass a considerable fortune.

And while he is most famous for being a business tycoon, he was also famous for being a savvy investor in the early American stock market. His investment philosophy was not based on greed or ambition. As a matter of fact, he would go on to become known as one of the greatest philanthropists in American history. It is estimated that he donated about $9.5 billion of his wealth to charitable organizations.

Andrew Carnegie is a hallmark of how investing in a business can make you rich. As discussed earlier, most investors are not seeking to actively participate in the administration of a business. Most investors are looking to take a passive role by investing in businesses and thereby generate income through passive investing.

But just like Ken Langone, understanding which businesses have the potential for growth is as much an art as it is a science. Andrew Carnegie had the foresight to understand how important the steel industry would become during the Industrial Age in America. It's safe to say that if he had decided to spend his time and efforts in a different industry, he wouldn't have become the tycoon that he eventually became.

By understanding that American industrial expansion required steel, he was able to capitalize on a singular market opportunity. This exemplifies how each period in history offers opportunities for individuals to become wealthy by taking part in up-and-coming Industries and businesses.

In hindsight, those who got in early on the internet and internet-based businesses were visionaries as they were able to see how the internet would revolutionize the world as we know it. The same goes for Carnegie. He had the foresight in understanding how steel would not only enable the development of industry itself but also would become a fundamental element of the automobile industry.

The main lesson from Andrew Carnegie is that wealthy individuals are not necessarily bred in the stock market. They can also come from the business world. By understanding how businesses can potentially become successful, you can find opportunities to get in while those businesses are still in their initial phases. If you manage to get in during this phase, you can truly become rich when the business becomes successful.

Chapter 7: Governance

Financial markets, or the business world for that matter, are highly complex systems that need governance and regulation.

Now, I understand that too much regulation is not a good thing. However, ground rules are needed in order to ensure that proper functioning is ensured.

The rules governing financial markets are set by law. These laws apply to the institutions that make up each market and may vary from country to country.

In the United States, there are local and federal laws and regulations which must be observed when investing. While this book is not a guide to corporate law, we will look into some of the foundations of governance.

But first, it is important that you, as an investor, seek professional advice and legal counsel regarding your rights and obligations. It is of the utmost importance that you understand how the rules apply to you. Otherwise, you might make a mistake which may end up costing you money, or even time in prison.

That being said, governance has a dual role. This dual role applies to both investors and brokers.

As such, there are sets of rules: one set that applies to financial institutions and one set that applies to individual investors.

In general, the purpose of an individual investor is to make as much money as possible. As such, individual investors are asked to comply with the procedures outlined in applicable legislation in the same manner that financial institutions are required.

In the case of financial institutions, they have a larger number of requirements they are obligated to comply with since their activities involved larger amounts of capital and regulate potentially fraudulent activity.

If you have followed stock markets for any period of time, you can see how there have been many cases of fraud, or corrupt practices. Therefore, legislation is enacted in order to address illegal practices.

When discussing market regulation, there is a "before" and "after."

The "before" refers to the time before the enactment of the Glass-Steagall Act of 1933. The US Congress passed this act at the time in order to close the loopholes and shut down the irresponsible, illegal and even fraudulent activity that led to the market crash of 1929.

One of the core issues address by Glass-Steagall was insider trading.

Insider trading consists of executives inside a publicly traded company, who have insider knowledge of a company's financial position, exploit that privileged position for their own benefit.

One good example of the insider trading is known as "pump and dump." Pump and dump schemes are those in which company executives fudge a company's financial position by not being forthcoming with regard to the company's financial situation. In some extreme cases, executives have gone as far as forging accounting ledgers and financial statements in order to present a healthy financial position.

Consequently, stock prices for that company rise. The insiders purchase their own company's stock while it is on the rise. But since they are perfectly aware of the company's financial position, they will get rid of the stock before the company implodes.

So, the "pump" part is where insiders artificially manipulate a company's financial position, so stock prices go up. Then, the "dump" part comes when the insiders sell their stock. The unsuspecting buyers think they are getting into a great deal only to learn that they were fooled when the company goes under. When the company eventually goes under, the shareholders of that company are left with worthless stock certificates.

One great example of this is Enron. Enron was an energy company that dabbled in oil, natural gas, and electricity. The executive of that company led a pump and dump scheme that lined their pockets full of cash and left shareholders absolutely broke. The worst part of this scheme was that these executives invested their employees' pension fund in its stock. When Enron tanked, the employee pension fund evaporated.

The Enron case highlights how markets are prone to manipulation and why regulation is needed to avoid such activity.

In 1929 though, regulation was much looser. Than allowed greedy investors to manipulate prices, issuance of shares and ultimately dumping them on an unsuspecting public. The end result was the largest crash in history.

The Glass-Steagall Act also created what is now known as the Securities and Exchange Commission (SEC). The SEC is the regulatory body that oversees the regulation of financial markets in the United States. Countries all around the world have similar entities, though their size, role, and power may vary from country to country.

The SEC has played a central role since 1933 in policing financial markets.

When Enron tanked in 2001, the SEC investigated the alleged charges of fraud. The company's top executives were subsequently arrested and convicted on fraud charges.

In essence, Glass-Steagall was meant to protect all players in financial markets by outlawing one very important practice that fueled the 1929 crash: the ability of banks to become both retail and investment banks.

Let's make a quick stop here.

Under Glass-Steagall and bank could not offer savings and loans products to customers while simultaneously dabble in financial markets.

So, if a bank had retail practices, that is, offered savings and loans products to customers, they could not turn around and offer them investment vehicles that the bank itself managed. The best retail banks could do what offer mutual funds which would then be placed under the management of an investment institution.

What this separation of investment and retail banking achieved was the elimination of an inherent conflict of interest. This conflict of interest stems from a bank's ability to monopolize markets. If a bank grew too big, it could jeopardize the entire financial system if it went under.

Glass-Steagall was repealed in 1999.

This meant that banks could engage in both investment and retail activities. The end result of this was that larger banks began buying up smaller, local banks. This led to a significant concentration of banks whereby large banks scooped up more and more of the public's money.

And, this also led to the financial crisis of 2008.

In essence, the financial crisis of 2008 was nothing more than banks dipping their toes into risky investment practices. For the sake of brevity, the repeal of Glass-Steagall allowed banks to both take deposits from customers and then turn around and issue mortgages.

Given the economic conditions of the time, money was abundant in the US banking system. However, hedge funds began buying into what are called "mortgage-backed securities" (MBS). MBSs provided a solid return that was virtually guaranteed never to fail since it was backed by the mortgaged properties themselves.

Here is where the tricky part comes in.

When hedge funds realized that banks were making money hand over first in the mortgage market, they asked the banks for a piece of the score. This is where banks taped a bunch of mortgages together, got a credit-rating agency to certify them as good, and off they went to hedge funds.

The hedge funds made loads of money since the loans were high quality and the debtors paid up.

Here comes the fork in the road.

Throughout this book, we have talked about how the average investor is not driven by greed, but by the desire to make as much money as possible in order to achieve financial freedom. Well, hedge funds have no such motivation. Hedge funds are driven to make more and more money.

So, banks began loosening their screening of loan applicants and got into the now-infamous sub-prime mortgages. A sub-prime mortgage is nothing more than a mortgage given to a person with a poor credit score. Under tighter standards, they wouldn't have qualified. But under the looser conditions, they passed with flying colors. And, off went the MBSs that hedge funds fed on.

The whole house of cards came crashing down when the borrowers began defaulting on their house payments. Foreclosures piled up, and the rest is history.

In the aftermath of the 2008 financial crisis, the Dodd-Frank Financial Regulatory Reform Act was passed by Congress in the United States in 2010. Also, other countries tightened up their banking regulations in order to avoid another such crisis in other parts of the world.

Today, lending practices have gotten a lot stricter. But the underlying threat remains as banks keep getting bigger and investors keep getting thirstier for returns.

Legislation governing brokers

The previous discussion highlights the importance of having legislation that is able to regulate banking and investment practices successfully.

As a result of the examples presented, regulations for traders are rather tough. Here is a quick list of some of the current legal instruments applicable to stock traders:

- The Securities Act of 1933 (not to be confused with Glass-Steagall)
- The Securities Exchange Act of 1934.
- Trust Indenture Act of 1939.
- Investment Company Act of 1940.

- Investment Advisors Act of 1940.
- Securities Investor Protection Act of 1970 (SIPA).
- Sarbanes-Oxley Act of 2002 (as a response to the Enron scandal)
- Dodd-Frank Wall Street Reform and Consumer Protection Act of 2010.

It's worth noting that a number of provisions contained in Dodd-Frank have been repealed since its enactment. The Act still stands, but it has grown from a 2,500-page document to over 22,000 pages. Thus, the study of this Act is nothing short of a full-time job.

In addition, the agency in charge of enforcing this legislation is the SEC. The SEC has the power to shut down any financial institution suspected of illegal activities and charge individual investors of fraud. Critics of the SEC have pointed out that is has lacked the fortitude to send big-time banking executives to jail. However, the SEC has a consistent track record of bringing fraudster to justice.

I would encourage you to do your homework and read up on this legislation. It will help you get a better understanding of the waters you will be navigating in. Although, day traders are not held accountable to these laws since they are considered individual investors. Nevertheless, your trading activities will most likely go through a duly supervised financial institution. That is why it is important to have a clear understanding of where you stand.

Legislation applicable to investors

With regard to individual investors, applicable legislation is the same as that which governs brokers and financial institutions. This is why it's best to become familiar with the terms of the legislation in order to avoid making mistakes and risking severe penalties.

In short, investors need to worry about avoiding anything fraudulent or illegal. Beyond that, the best thing that investors can do is make sure that they keep good records in case anything should happen. Moreover, it's always good to check out what financial institutions you are doing business with especially if you are unfamiliar with them or never heard of them before.

I would encourage you to seek legal advice in case you are unfamiliar with anything stated in contracts or legal documentation.

One other thing: if you should ever suspect that anyone you are doing business with may be engaging in risky activities, seek legal advice. If any business associates are engaging in fraudulent or illegal activities, and it can be proven that you knew about it, you could be on the hook, too.

Tax considerations

Regarding taxes, it's best that you seek professional advice on this matter. Taxes can be complex and often require specialized knowledge. In the long run, it might be best to consult with a professional accountant or a CPA to make sure that you are complying with local and federal tax laws.

In addition, full-time traders fall under a different tax system since they are neither employees nor self-employed. It's vitally important to also plan out a solid tax strategy along with your investment strategy in order to make that you are not running the IRS afoul. Mistakes with taxes can be costly and may even result in legal trouble.

Chapter 8: How to Win the Stock Market Game

In this chapter, we're going to be looking at some additional investment strategies that can help you get ahead of the stock market game. So far, we've discussed the number of important elements associated with investment strategy. However, the four strategies that we will discuss in this chapter are often overlooked by investors.

These four strategies are designed to help you gain a clearer understanding of how you can transform the strategies which we have previously described into much more successful overall investment approaches.

As stated earlier, an investment strategy is based on investor expectations. For the purpose of this book, we're considering a much more conservative investment strategy since we do not advocate risky investment practices.

The goal of a conservative investment strategy is to enable investors to firstly make enough income to fund their lifestyle and pay for their basic needs. Once basic needs are covered, investors can move on to bigger and better things.

That being said, bigger and better things can be achieving true financial freedom.

One important note is that the strategies described in this chapter are focused more on maximizing value and return with regard to the amount invested. That is, to maximize the return on investment based on the cost of each investment made.

So, let's take a closer look at each one of these investment strategies.

Value investing

The first strategy we're going to discuss in this chapter is called value investing.

Value investing consists in an investment strategy which seeks to acquire stocks that are being traded for less than their Book value. That being said, it is important to define the difference between book value and market value.

First, a stock's book value is that which is reported on a company's balance sheet. All publicly traded companies have a book value, that is, the real value of shares based on a company's balance sheet. This book value is calculated by the sum of all of the company's physical and non-physical assets. Examples of physical assets can be machinery, inventories of goods, office equipment, and so on.

Non-physical assets can include patents, intellectual property, or any other non-tangible assets included in its balance sheet.

A company's liabilities offset these assets. In other words, liabilities are nothing more than two companies' obligations or debt to be paid.

The end result of this consideration is called a company's equity. That is assets (-) liabilities = equity.

Let's consider an example:

ABC Company's total assets amount to $100. Also, ABC Company has $75 worth of liabilities. Thus, ABC's equity is $25.

Now, let's also assume that ABC Company has 10 outstanding shares. That means we must divide ABC Company's $25 Equity by its 10 outstanding shares. The result works out to a share price of $2.50. Consequently, ABC company's book value on its shares is $2.50.

Assuming that ABC Company is a successful company, it is producing healthy results and paying investors a good profit; investors will seek to purchase shares of ABC Company. This implies that ABC Company's shares are in demand and as mentioned earlier when demand exceeds supply, the price will go up.

In this regard, investors consider that ABC Company's shares are worth $5 each. This is the shares' market value. It is called "market value" since it is what investors are willing to pay to acquire these shares. In this example, ABC Company shares are worth double their book value. That is $5 market value as compared to $2.50 book value.

Now, let's assume another scenario:

We continue to assume that ABC company shares are worth $2.50. However, the shares market value stands at $2. This means that ABC company shares are traded on the market for less than their Book value.

This can be due to many reasons. For instance, ABC Company is relatively new on the market and has not caught investors' attention. Another reason might be that the company has underperformed lately and so, investors believe that it is not a worthwhile investment. This has led the shares market value to drop below its book value.

This is where value investment comes in.

A savvy investor may realize that ABC Company's subpar performance was not due to its inability to produce good results, but rather it was due to factors beyond its control, and so, investors unjustly punished ABC Company by dumping the stock.

This is a classic example of a buy low, sell high proposition.

As an investor, if you are able to spot such an opportunity, you may put yourself in the position to clean up and make a significant profit. You may have to hold on to the stock for longer than you would like to and hope that the company will rebound — however, a word of caution. If the stock falls any further, it is time for you to sell immediately and cut your losses. On the other hand, if the stock suddenly rises, it is time for you to sell immediately because you cannot be assured that the stock will continue to rise indefinitely.

Value stocks out there. Some of which were known as penny stocks. Penny stocks derive their name because share prices are worth less than a dollar each. In a broader sense, penny stocks refer to value investing. In order to find hidden gems, you will have to invest time and research into finding such hidden gems. Nevertheless, the potential gains which can be made through value investing may well offset the time and effort needed to find them.

Growth investing

Another useful strategy for investors is one known as growth investing. This type of investing consists of purchasing shares of a company and holding on to them while that company's capital, or equity, continues to grow. Growth investing requires a keen understanding of a company's internal structure and value proposition to its customers. Often, growth investing comes from companies which are underachievers or have not hit their stride yet.

Growth investing doesn't necessarily have to happen in the stock market. Growth investors may seek to invest in privately held companies much the same way that venture capitalists do with startups.

Let's consider an example:

ABC Company is in its start-up phase. The founders of this company are looking to acquire financing in order to expand their operations. And so, they have reached out to banks and venture capitalists. This first round of financing calls for an investment of $1,000. The founders of ABC Company have decided that they need that money in order to finance the purchase of equipment needed to expand their operations.

So, venture capitalists have decided to invest in ABC Company since they feel the value proposition offered by this company will ultimately pay off. In exchange for the $1,000 in financing, the founders of ABC Company are willing to surrender

25% of their company's control. In this example, 25% of the equity stake in ABC Company is worth $1,000.

Since the potential for growth of ABC Company looks pretty good, investors have decided to hold on to the stock as the company grows. Indeed, ABC Company has taken off. Sales have increased, and their name recognition has grown solid in their market.

The book value of an ABC Company stock was $4,000 when Venture capitalists bought. This can be inferred by considering that 25% equals $1,000 and that 25% is ¼ of ABC Company's total equity. So, $1000 multiplied by 4 gives us a total of $4,000.

As such, ABC Company's Book value of $4,000 at the time of the first round of investing has grown to $8,000. This growth is the result of solid business practices and organic growth as seen in the company's increased market share and profits. At this point, venture capitalists have decided that it is time to sell their stake in ABC Company and they have found another group of investors who are willing to pay for the shares according to their new book value.

Since ABC Company's capital has doubled, the venture capitalists' stake in the company is now worth $2,000. They agreed to sell and collect $2,000. This implies that the venture capitalists have made a profit of $1,000

In this example, investors did not make a speculative investment in the stock market assuming that the price of shares would go up based on market forces. This example highlights that there is much money to be made in investing in private firms. Furthermore, publicly traded companies may offer individual investors the opportunity to buy stock directly from them. This type of transaction is a means of bypassing the need for a broker or brokerage firm.

So, it is well worth the effort to do some research and find out if publicly traded companies offer direct purchase plans, or if there are private companies out there seeking financing from investors.

Income investing

The third strategy in this chapter is called income investing or investing for income.

In this approach, investors are looking to allocate investments in such a way that Investments produce a steady income over time. Income investors are essentially looking for a source of income that will help fund their lifestyle.

As opposed to traditional stock trading which looks to flip equities for a profit and which do not represent a steady stream of income, income investors are working to make safer investments on assets which will produce income over time.

One classic example of this type of investing is real estate. Real estate investors buy properties which they can rent out and provide them with a steady stream of income at the end of every month. It goes without saying, that real estate has its own set of risks and may not prove to be as profitable as investing in equities. Furthermore, real estate requires a considerable amount of upfront investment in terms of time and money.

Investors who are looking for a steady stream of income and who are not keen on devoting a considerable amount of time and money toward researching and involving themselves in the administration of their assets can choose from a wide range of financial instrument to suit their needs. We have discussed several of these instruments. Nevertheless, we will go over them once again in order to pinpoint a solid financial strategy.

The safest income producing assets out there are bonds. The myriad type of bonds available is highlighted by the government, or sovereignty, which offers the lowest risk and also the lowest returns. Unless a country is at higher risk of default, you can be sure that a country will own up to its debt obligation and make the payment of bonds plus interest effective. In order to maintain their steady flow of income, investors may choose to roll over their bonds and collect the interest paid out by them at a given point in time.

Another type of investment that produces income on a regular basis is a certificate of deposit. Certificates of deposit produce a yield in the form of interest and may be paid out according to the terms of the investment. These terms could be monthly or annually. Furthermore, an investor may choose to allocate investable funds into a mortgage-backed certificate of deposit. Unlike mortgage-backed securities, mortgage-backed certificates of deposit are those in which banks collect funds from the public in order to finance mortgages for their customers.

Also, Investors may choose to buy stock in either public or privately held companies. The plan here is not to trade the stock when the prices go up or down. Investor logic, in this case, would be based upon the dividends produced by the company. This dividend, or yield, on each share, will provide a type of income that investors can collect annually, or at any other point in time.

Another type of income investing strategy is an annuity. As indicated earlier, annuities are a type of investment that functions much like traditional insurance. Annuities pay out a fixed monthly or annual payment at the maturity of the annuity. This is a great investment strategy for folks who are looking to finance their retirement. The only care that needs to be taken when considering an annuity is that annuities only payout for the time specified in the contract. So, if an annuity will make monthly payments for 20 years, there is a possibility that the investor outlives their annuity. Consequently, an investor may choose to delay collection on the annuity as long as possible.

Passive investing

The final type of investment strategy discussed in this chapter corresponds to passive investing.

Passive investing means that investors will allocate their investible funds into investment vehicles that will generate an income, produce dividends, pay interest, or any other type a profit in which the investor does not have any type of participation whatsoever.

The classic example of a passive investing is royalties. Royalties are fixed payments that are made during specified periods of time and are derived from the ownership of rights to intellectual property or patents. For example, book authors collect royalties on the sales of their books long after their book was originally written and published. Likewise, Musicians and artists royalties on their artistic works for many years after these works have been published.

The average investor may choose to implement a passive income strategy. Much like incoming investing, passive investing's main purpose is to provide investors with a steady stream of income. The difference between income and passive investing is the passive investing does not involve the investor in any way other than the initial investment itself.

One great example of passive investing is buying into a privately-owned company. This is commonly referred to as being a silent partner. Silent partners will provide funding for a business but will not actively participate in the management of the business in any way. Silent partners often hold seats on boards but only in a representative role. They may have voice, but no vote or they may have voice and vote but are only required to be present at specific board meetings.

Another type of passive investing through business ownership is through the purchase of franchises. Franchises are business structures that have already been set up in such a way that investors don't need to develop the business itself in any way. Franchises offer a business structure that has already been proven to be successful. Consequently, an investor will pay the corresponding fees and royalties for the use of the business model. In return, the franchise owner will collect profits derived from that business' operation.

Another great way to engage in passive investing is through the purchase of ETFs. As described earlier ETFs are funds which pool investor money and gamble in an underlying asset or security. As such, investors only need to pay into the ETF and collect their earnings at the point specified in the contract. For instance, oil ETFs have oil as their underlying asset. The ETF managers will trade in oil while the investor is not required to do anything. The ETF's earnings are dependent on the price of oil since this is the commodity which the ETF is based on.

There are myriads of ETFs available. Therefore, investors would do well to research into the different types of ETFs available and choose the one that best fits their expectations and investment approach. For the purpose of passive investment, ETFs provide a great opportunity to buy into a fund which does not require much work beyond periodic revisions of that funds' performance.

Chapter 9: Advanced Trading Strategies

Congratulations on making it this far in the book. I must admit it's been a pretty amazing journey. I hope you have enjoyed reading this book as much as I have enjoyed writing it. A lot of time and research has gone into producing the pages that you have just read.

But hold on!

We still have one more chapter to go.

In this chapter, we will be looking at three riskiest types of investment approaches that an average investor can engage in. This is why we have left them for last.

Throughout this book, we have encouraged a conservative investment strategy. The reason for this is that risky practices require investors to have more skill and experience. Risk is an often-overlooked factor due to investors' ambition.

Nevertheless, we will be discussing riskier propositions so that you can get an idea of how you can dip your toes into a more exciting facet of stock investing.

One word of caution before proceeding: anytime you engage in a higher risk investment strategy it is important for you to do your homework and cover your back. That being said, if something should go wrong and you take a considerable hit to your investments, you may end up losing a considerable amount of money, if not everything.

With that in mind, let's move on and look into the next three strategies which can help you make considerable gains in a short period of time.

Short selling

An investment lingo, you will often hear you the terms "long" and "short."

In essence, a long position is when you own the underlying asset that is being traded.

For example, I am selling a car. I am the registered owner of the vehicle, and I hold all rights to it. Since I have chosen to sell it, interested buyers will have the assurance that I am selling something which is legally mine. Consequently, the proceeds from this sale may result in a profit or a loss to me.

On the other hand, short selling consists in selling an asset which you do not own.

You might ask yourself: how is it possible to sell an asset which you do not own?

Well, the answer is quite simple.

Consider selling a car as an example. I can sell a car which I do not own if a customer comes to me and asks me to sell their car for them. Since I own a large lot of used cars, I have the infrastructure needed to advertise the car and provide interested buyers with the advice they need in order to purchase the car.

Now, considering that I am not the legal owner of the car, the proceeds from the sale of the car do not belong to me. They belong to the rightful owner of the car. The way that I would make money in this type of deal is by charging a commission. The owner of the car and I have agreed on the sale price. From the total sale price, a certain percentage of that would go to the owner. The remaining portion belongs to me as my commission.

Just like selling a car for someone else, short selling, or short positions, are positions that investors take in selling equities that belong to another person. This proposition becomes riskier than traditional investing since it implies that the equities and securities will be sold at a given price in the market.

Short selling also implies a binding contract which holds both ends accountable for the result of the transactions made. Stockholders who wish to sell, but not sell the stock themselves, will choose to go through a broker. The broker, in this case, will go to the market and find buyers for that particular security. The binding contract between both parties holds the broker accountable to pay a certain amount of money to the shareholders. In this example, the broker makes money off the commissions derived from a profitable sale of stocks.

However, short selling gets even riskier when an investor chooses to bet that a stock will fall in price. When to stock falls in price, the investor makes money when they turn around and sell the stock for a higher price.

The issue with short selling is that investors may lose considerable amounts of money if the stock rises in value after the investor has placed a short position. At this point, an investor must immediately buy the stock and cover their position. Otherwise, if the stock continues to increase in value, the loss will become greater.

It's important to note, that investors who short stocks are essentially betting on a stock's price going down. Since these investors don't actually own the stock, they must buy it at some point in order to deliver the shares that were sold to the buyer.

This type of trading requires investors to have buyers and sellers of the shorted stock on hold so they can make an immediate transaction based on results of share prices.

Let's consider this example:

ABC Company's current market value stands at $10 a share. An investor considers that the share price will fall. This motivates the investor to put in a short position. At this point, the investor has not purchased anything yet. However, they are on the hook for fluctuations in the price of that stock.

This investor has not purchased any of ABC Company shares but sells them to another investor at $10 a share. The short selling magic occurs ABC Company's share price falls drastically. Let's assume it crashes to $5 a share. The investor has collected $10 from another buyer but is obligated to deliver those shares to the buyer. When the share price crashes, the investor will go and purchase the actual shares at $5 apiece. Subsequently, the investor must deliver them to the original buyer who paid $10 per share. In this example, the investor cleaned up because the buyer who purchased shares ended up taking the loss when the share price fell to the floor. The investor made a killing since he was able to buy the shares at a lower price before being obligated to deliver them to the buyer.

The strategy can quickly backfire when share prices go up after an investor has chosen to put in a short position. Considering the previous example, ABC Company's share price rose from $10 per share to $11. The buyer has paid $10 per share. The investor now will be forced to purchase the shares that must be delivered to the buyer at $11 apiece. That represents a $1 loss per share.

Needless to say, this strategy is very risky since markets are often unpredictable and conditions can change at any time. Furthermore, this strategy is ideal for insider trading and can lead the criminal charges.

so, if you choose to engage in short selling proceed with caution.

Buying on margin

The next strategy discussed in this chapter is called "buying on margin."

Buying on margin essentially means that an investor borrows money in order to invest in a security or an asset.

One example of this could be taking out a bank loan in order to invest in the stock market. This is typically done by people who do not have funds to invest but wish to do so in hopes that they can clean up without actually investing anything.

This is how it works:

An investor borrows a sum of money. Let's assume $1,000. The investor then proceeds to invest the $1,000 into shares of a given number of companies. The biggest constraint that an investor faces is the moment when the loan needs to be repaid. Let's assume that this $1,000 loan needs to be repaid at the end of the month. This gives the investor 30 days for the $1,000 investment to grow.

If all goes well, the investor will collect more than $1,000 at the end of the month. The investor then repays the initial $1,000 loan and pockets the rest.

An investor on margin can make a killing if their initial investment grows exponentially. For the sake of this example, let's assume that that $1,000 investment has grown to $100,000. Magically, the investor has made a profit of $99,000 in a one-month period. All the investor needs to do is return the $1,000 and keep the rest.

Now, Let's assume the worst-case scenario.

The investor borrows the same $1,000 and invests it into a series of stocks. The market has crashed, and that $1,000 investment has evaporated. Now the investor is stuck with a $1,000 debt and may not be able to repay it. In short, this is like gambling at a casino except you're gambling with someone else's money.

Investing on margin is what wiped out a great deal of investors during the market crash of 1929. Since the stock market was in a huge bubble, investors took out loans on their homes or any other assets they could use as collateral in order to invest in the stock market. Some cleaned up, and those that stayed in the market too long were wiped out by the crash. Needless to say, many investors lost everything and ended up living on the street. This led to mass suicides of investors who have lost everything.

Therefore, investing on margin is not for the faint of heart. It requires a great deal of experience and skill in financial markets. Since it is virtually impossible to time markets, it is very unlikely that investing on margin can come without risk. Considering this type of investment is essentially gambling with someone else's money, great precaution needs to be taken. In the event that an investor loses on an investment, they will still be on the hook for the repayment of the loan.

This is why the derivatives market poses such a significant risk to the overall health of the world's financial system. Many of the transactions conducted in the derivatives markets are done on margin. Often, these deals are closed with a handshake. And while there may be legal contracts that bind all parties to their obligations, they're still gambling at a stock that will rise or fall, that a company will go bankrupt, or even bet on an IPO.

As such, margin investing is not recommended for everyone, and great care must be taken in order to be as sure as possible that investments made on margin will at least yield enough to cover the margin call.

Portfolio Management

The final strategy discussed in this chapter pertains to portfolio management.

This activity is where an individual manages investments and assets on behalf of other investors. This type of activity is generally the livelihood of stockbrokers and traders.

However, individual investors, through the use of an online trading platform, may choose to pool the money of other individuals an invest it. Typically, this type of investing is done with funds from close friends and family.

It goes without saying that this is a risky activity since making wrong investments may lead to significant losses thereby leaving a portfolio manager in serious trouble. In addition, it is technically illegal to engage in this type of activity which may even lead to criminal charges.

Consequently, any time an individual engages in managing other people's money, it opens the door to a potential disaster.

Hedge funds typically invest in this manner. And as stated earlier, hedge funds tend to engage in risky investment practices. Moreover, hedge funds are clubs of wealthy people who pool their resources together in order to make money based on the expertise of a money manager. If the manager makes a mistake, it is safe to say that the investors will not be pleased.

The safest bet is to apply for a brokerage license. It requires an investment of time and effort. Nevertheless, obtaining a license can not only open employment doors, but it can give you the edge you need in order to become a successful day trader.

Conclusion

Well, we made it to the end of the line. Thank you for taking the time to go through this book.

The next step is to put everything into practice. I encourage you to look into an online investment platform which offers a free training account. With this training account, you can get your feet wet. You can feel free to cut loose. After all, you won't lose anything if you make a couple of bad deals. In fact, you will have everything to gain since the experience you will earn is priceless.

I also encourage you to dig deeper and further your learning on the topics discussed in this book. It's worth the time and effort to become a true master of the financial markets and instruments we have discussed.

One final word of caution: always seek professional advice when you are unsure about anything. Uncertainty breeds mistakes and mistakes may end up becoming costly. So, it pays to spend a couple of bucks and seek advice from qualified individuals who can point you in the right direction.

I hope that you have found this book to be useful and informative. It is the result of years of knowledge and experience which have been condensed into this single volume. I also hope that you can become a multiplier of this knowledge. Please share this information with your friends and family, or anyone you think might be interested in becoming an investor.

As always, please don't forget to leave a review. In doing so, you will be helping other folks who might be interested in purchasing this book. Your honest opinion will be greatly appreciated and useful.

Thank you once again and happy trading!

Finally, if you found this book useful in any way, a review on Amazon is always appreciated!